America's Best History Timeline

from the Staff at
americasbesthistory.com

Disclaimer: The information provided within this timeline was gleaned from various sources, as well as the knowledge and experience of the America's Best History staff, and should not be considered a scholarly work per se, but as a jumping off point for the reader to go into more detail about a particular topic of their interest. We would also urge you to visit the historic sites of the USA, as they will provide you with invaluable knowledge and experience into our history, no matter which subject or site you prefer. It is often the best way to add to your historic wealth of knowledge, and a whole lot more fun than you might anticipate.

It should also be understood by the reader that providing specific dates, particularly for events prior to 1850, is often difficult and subject to change when new information and documents emerge. And, even then, those documents can include recollections from participants at the time that may or may not be accurate. Take that into account with the realization that the sequence of events can provide a perspective to history that can supercede the actual dates anyway, although the actual dates do provide a context and meaning as well.

America's Best History Timeline

from americasbesthistory.com

TABLE OF CONTENTS

America's Best History Timeline

from americasbesthistory.com

Timeline of Pre-Revolution America 1400's

August 3, 1492 - After years of negotiations to get the funds to make his journey, Christopher Columbus sets out on three ships, the Niña, the Pinta, and the Santa Maria, to find a westward passage to the Indies under the auspices of Queen Isabella I of Spain.

October 12, 1492 - Rodrigo de Triana, a crew member of the Pinta, sights the land of the Americas in the Bahamas. This was the first of four voyages Christopher Columbus would make under the patent of the Spanish and Isabella I of Castile. It began the period of Spanish colonization of the New World. Columbus called the Bahamian site, San Salvador. He would also explore the islands of Cuba and Haiti on this trip, but not the continent of North America itself.

September 24, 1493 - Columbus began his second trip to the American colonies with seventeen ships and 1,200 men. These men were meant to colonize the land found and claimed during the journey beyond the few left in the Americas after the first voyage. He would arrive in the New World again on November 3, 1493 and explore more of the islands in the Caribbean, including Puerto Rico and the Dominican Republic.

June 7, 1494 - The Treaty of Tordesillas, between Spain and Portugal, attempts to ratify and clarify ownership of the lands outside Europe and who could claim them. This was an effort to resolve questions arising from the return of Columbus. This treaty, and a subsequent treaty on April 22, 1529, the Treaty of Zaragosa, would only further confuse the issue beyond the two nations Spain and Portugal.

March 5, 1496 - King Henry VII signs an agreement with John (Giovanni) Cabot to explore the western hemisphere under the flag and authority of England. It is thought likely that the British King was in disagreement with the Treaty of Tordesillas, as well as a prior Papal decision, to effectively split the riches and exploration of the New Worlds between Spain and Portugal. He would attempt a first voyage with one ship, but be unsuccessful, and turn back.

May 2, 1497 - On his second voyage for England from the port of Bristol, John Cabot (aka Giovanni, a Genoese native sailing under the English flag) rediscovers the North American continent on June 24, 1497, the first European exploration of the continent since Norse explorers in the 11th century. He explores the northeast coast, landing first at Cape Bonavista in Newfoundland. They made landfall for a short period of time to raise the English flag, then explored the coast. His ship was known as the Matthew of Bristol.

May 1498 - Cabot undertakes another voyage to the New World under his English papers. It is unknown whether Cabot returned from this voyage and various reports state that his ships were lost at sea. Recent research suggests a second theory, that his ships did return to England after a two year exploration of the coastline of Canada and the United States, even down into the Spanish claimed territories of Columbus in the Caribbean.

May 30, 1498 - The third voyage of Columbus began in the Spanish city of Sanlucar. During this voyage, he explored the islands of the Caribbean again as well as the South American territories of what is now Venezuela. Upon visiting the previously established settlements, he found much discontent among those left behind to colonize the region.

Timeline of Pre-Revolution America 1500's

1500: Indian culture flourishes in Florida as exemplified by the woodcarving in the Calusa culture. The Calusa had been living in this area for 1,000 years prior to European contact.

May 11, 1502 - Christopher Columbus left Spain on his fourth voyage to the New World, landing back on the islands of Martinique and Jamaica in June. This voyage would take him to Central America, but not to North America.

1507 - The native population on the island of Hispaniola among the Taino population is decimated when European disease begins to affect the native population. Several epidemics of smallpox over the first fifty years after European settlement saw a decrease in their population from hundreds of thousands to less than five hundred.

March 4, 1513 - Ponce de Leon leaves Puerto Rico to explore the coast of Florida, looking for the Fountain of Youth. There were two hundred men and three ships undertaking the exploration.

April 2, 1513 - Ponce de Leon sites land near St. Augustine, coming ashore the next day and claiming the land for Spain. He names the land La Florida, after the Easter season Festival of Flowers.

1524 - Giovanni da Verrazano enters New York harbor during a French expedition from the Carolinas to Nova Scotia. It is regarded by many as the first European exploration of the Atlantic seaboard of North America (assuming John Cabot did not return from his last voyage there) since the Norse expeditions five hundred years earlier.

June 17, 1527 - The Narváez expedition leaves Spain to explore and colonize Spanish Florida under the command of Pánfilo de Narváez. There were 600 members of the expedition.

April 12, 1528 - After much hardship and stops in the Caribbean, the Narváez expedition reaches Florida near Tampa Bay and debarks two days later in Boca Ciega Bay, where they encounter natives of the Safety Harbor region. For the next four years, the expedition met a dire fate due to battles with natives (Timucua, Apalachee, and Tocobaga), the sea, and starvation. The expedition had split into several forces by the end of this year, and in total, slightly more than eighty members of the original expedition had survived, some reaching the Galveston, Texas area by boat.

April 22, 1529 - The Treaty of Zaragosa attempts to clarify the Treaty of Tordesillas from 1494 between Spain and Portugal. Again this treaty attempted to clarify previous boundaries agreed between only two nations, Spain and Portugal, plus earlier boundaries by the papacy. All lands would still be divided between the two nations, with the Philippines and North America to Spain, and the Moluccas to Portugal.

1532 - Four men associated with the original Narváez expedition attempt to reach posts of the Spanish Empire in Mexico. These men were Álvar Núñez Cabeza de Vaca, Alonso del Castillo Maldonado, Andrés Dorantes de Carranza, and a slave, Estevanico. They became the first men from Europe and Africa to enter the American west, traveling across Texas, New Mexico, and Arizona.

July 1536 - Survivors of the Narváez expedition reach fellow Spaniards near Sinaloa, Mexico.

May 25, 1539 - Hernando de Soto lands in Florida with nine ships and six hundred and twenty men at Shaw's Point in today's Bradenton, Florida, and begins to explore the interior of the Americas. They explored the western coast of Florida and encamped during the winter at Anhaica in Apalachee territory.

February 23, 1540 - Exploration of the southwest and western United States to California by European expeditions begins when Fernando Vasquez de Coronado departs Compostela, in present day Mexico, looking to conquer the Seven Cities of Gold. The two year expedition took him into the lands of the United States, into New Mexico and to the Grand Canyon. The expedition included 335 Spanish, 4 monks, and over 1,000 natives. During one scouting party, members of the expedition became the first

Europeans to discover the Grand Canyon.

1540-1541 - The first war between native Americans and Europeans in the southwest occurs between troops of Coronado and the Tiwa Indians. The Tiguex war was waged near Bernalillo, New Mexico against the dozen pueblos of the tribe on the American and Mexican sides of the Rio Grande River.

1540 - The de Soto expedition continues into Georgia in search for gold and a passage west. He would proceed into the mountains of North Carolina and Tennessee. An ambush in northern Alabama, which may have been precipitated by actions of the expedition, by the Mabilian Indian tribe, resulted in twenty Spanish explorer deaths and the demise of thousands of Indian warriors. De Soto burned the city. He would later winter near Tupelo, Mississippi.

1541 - The Coronado expedition continues to search for the city of Quivara and traverses the states of Arizona, New Mexico, Texas, and Oklahoma until their final destination near Lyons, Kansas. At this time, they were only a few hundred miles from the exploration by de Soto.

May 8, 1541 - After a Chicasaw raid earlier in the year, de Soto's expedition was in dire shape, however, they push forward, reaching the Mississippi River and becoming the first documented Europeans to witness it. Hernando de Soto led his expeditionary force across the Mississippi River and would explore Texas, Arkansas, and Oklahoma. This expedition lay claims to these territories for the Spanish. De Soto would die early in 1542.

1550-1551 - A debate over the treatment and status of Indians in the New World is held in Valladolid, Spain. The Valladolid debate pitted the Bishop of Chiapas, who stated that the American Indian was a free man deserving equal treatment to European colonists per theology. The opposite viewpoint, that Indians were natural slaves, was debated by a fellow Dominican, using claims of theology as well as natural law.

1564-1565 - A French colony is attempted in Florida by Rene de Laudonnière. It is located along the St. John's River, but is short-lived with expulsion by the Spanish holding its fate.

1564-1565 - The first known painting of American Indians by European colonists is made by French artist Jacques le Moyne.

September 8, 1565 - Spanish explorer Pedro Menéndez de Avilés, a Spanish admiral, founds St. Augustine, Florida. It is the first permanent settlement in the United States and serves as a military outpost and base for Catholic missionary settlements.

June 17, 1579 - Francis Drake claims the lands of California for Great Britain and Queen Elizabeth I. Drake is on his voyage around the world in the ship, the Golden Hand.

August 17, 1585 - Roanoke Island colony is founded by an expedition organized by Sir Walter Raleigh (Raleigh never visited North America himself) during his attempt to colonize the area of Virginia and North Carolina. The colony fails.

June 6, 1586 - The city of St. Augustine, Florida, is razed by Francis Drake.

1587 - A second try to colonize Roanoke Island is attempted by Sir Walter Raleigh under the governor John White. White came back to England to find more supplies, but his return was delayed due to the need for ships to fight the Spanish Armada.

August 18, 1590 - John White's return trip to the Roanoke Island Colony finds no signs of the colonists, beyond the words CROATOAN and CRO carved into tree trunks. The fate of its people is unknown to this date, and is often referred to as the "Lost Colony of Roanoke Island."

1600 - In present-day Arizona and New Mexico, members of the Franciscan order from the Spanish settlements in Mexico establish missions in Hopi Indian tribe areas. The first permanent mission, San Bernardino, was established at Awátobi in 1629.

April 26, 1607 - After five months at sea, three ships led by Captain Christopher Newport reach Cape Henry on the Virginia coast. The Susan Constant, the Discovery, and the Godspeed, later move up the James River for forty miles till they stop on Jamestown Island.

May 13, 1607 - The three ships land in Jamestown, establishing the first English settlement in the United States. There are 103 settlers among them. Upon arrival, Captain John Smith is named to the governing council.

September 3, 1609 - Henry Hudson, working for the Dutch, sails into New York harbor and up the river that would bear his name to Albany.

1609 - Exploration of the New World continues as Samuel de Champlain explores Lake Champlain.

April 5, 1614 - The history of Jamestown continues with the marriage of Pocahontas to John Rolfe, who would bring tobacco seeds to the colony and begin its harvesting this year. Their marriage led to eight years of peace among the colonists and Indians.

1600 to 1615 - American Indian Felipe Guaman Poma de Ayala (Quechua) illustrates his 1,189-page book, El primer nueva corónica, y buen gobierno.

1618 to 1619 - Smallpox epidemic wipes out 90% of the Native Americans in the Massachusetts Bay area.

July 30, 1619 - First representative assembly, the House of Burgesses, held in America is elected in Jamestown. The next month, the Dutch land with indentured servants in Jamestown.

November 11, 1620 - The Puritan expedition which left England for the New World on September 6, reaches Cape Cod near Provincetown, not their original destination of Virginia. They explore the coastline for an appropriate settlement location.

December 11, 1620 - A landing party searches the coast for a suitable site for a settlement and start to move the entire party to Plymouth Harbor. Plymouth Rock was identified as the first solid land the Pilgrims set foot on.

December 20, 1620 -The Purtitans begin to establish settlement in Plymouth. They form the Mayflower Compact, which established a government and legal structure. During the next winter, half of the colonists would perish. Site of the settlement had previously been the location of an Indian village that had been wiped out in 1617 by a plague.

September/October 1621 - The first Thanksgiving celebration is held in the autumn for three days between the Pilgrims and members of the Wampanoag tribe, who had helped them settle and plant the colony's land.

March 22, 1622 - The Indian Massacre of 1622 occurs when Chief Opchanacanough and the Powhatan Confederacy tried to rid the colony of settlers. One third of the colony at the time, three hundred people, were killed.

1623-1626 - In the area of New Mexico, on Navajo land, warriors of the Jemez Apache tribe war against Spaniards and Tiwas.

May 6, 1626 - Peter Minuit, one of eight men left by Dutch explorers headed for the Albany area from the ship New Netherland on Manhattan Island, buys the island from the Man-a-hat-a Indians for $24 in trinkets.

March 25, 1634 - Maryland is founded as a Catholic colony promoting religious tolerance. The subsequent state is named for Queen Henrietta Maria, wife of England's Charles I.

October 28, 1636 - Harvard College is founded in Cambridge, Massachusetts.

June 1636 - Providence, Rhode Island is founded as a colony by Roger Williams. Its charter would be granted eight years later as a democratic colony believing in the separation of church and state.

1640 - The first book is printed in North America, the Bay Psalm Book.

1641 - Witchcraft is made a capital crime in English law. The Massachusetts colony becomes the first colony to legalize slavery.

March 1, 1642 - York, Maine of the Massachusetts Colony (known as Georgeana in colonial times) becomes the first incorporated city in the American colonies.

1643 - The book, A Key into Language of Americas, is published by Roger Williams, co-founder of the Rhode Island colony.

April 18, 1644 - In the last Indian rebellion in the region, Opchanacanough and the Powhatan Indians attack the English at Jamestown, but their effort is repulsed and proves unsuccessful.

May 29, 1647 - The constitution of the General Assembly of Rhode Island is drafted, separating church and state, as well as permitting public referendums and initiatives in legislation.

1650 - Slavery is legalized in Connecticut and recognized in the American colonies.

June 9, 1650 - The Harvard Board becomes the first legalized corporation in the American colonies.

May 18, 1652 - Rhode Island passes the first law in the American colonies restricting slavery, making it illegal for more than ten years.

August 22, 1654 - Jewish settlement in the American colonies begins with the arrival of twenty-three settlers from Brazil in New Amsterdam.

September 13, 1660 - The Navigation act is passed by British Parliament to control colonial commerce in the New World.

September 8, 1664 - Three hundred British troops seize New Netherlands from the Dutch in a peaceful takeover. The Duke of York, brother to Charles II, is granted the Dutch province and city of New Amsterdam, renaming them New York.

September 6, 1667 – A large hurricane ravages southeast Virginia, with twelve days of rain, causing damage to plantation homes and crops.

August 9, 1673 - Dutch forces recapture the colony of New York (New Amsterdam) from the British, but would only be able to hold power in the area for one year.

September 19, 1676 - Bacon's Rebellion causes the burning of Jamestown. Nathanial Bacon leads the rebellion of planters against Governor Berkeley. Bacon would perish and twenty-three others were executed.

August 12, 1676 - The Indian War between the Narragansett Indians and the colonists in New England ends.

April 9, 1682 - France claims the lower Mississippi River valley, Louisiana, when Robert Cavelier, Sieur de LaSalle explores the region.

1683 - The colony of Pennsylvania is established when William Penn signs a treaty with the Delaware Indians and pays for Pennsylvania lands.

1684 - Additional outposts, at the behest of Cavelier, in Illinois and Texas spread the influence of the French in the central part of the American territories.

March 19, 1687 - Mutiny causes the death of Robert Cavelier, Sieur de LaSalle.

September 25, 1690 - The first newspaper issue in the United States publishes in Boston, the Public Occurrences. It was suppressed after its initial issue and the publication of a regular newspaper would not begin again until 1704.

1691 - The Plymouth colony, which had remained independent since its founding in 1620, joins the Massachusetts Bay Colony.

February 1692 - May 1693 - The Salem witch hunts, spurred by preaching, results in the arrest of one hundred and fifty people and the death of nineteen. These trials were held in Essex, Suffolk, and Middlesex counties.

1696 - Captain William Kidd becomes a pirate of the high seas, turning away from his job for the British Empire to patrol and control piracy. He would be hanged in 1701.

1699 - Jamestown is abandoned after the statehouse is burned. Colonial government was moved to Middle Plantation, renamed soon after as Williamsburg.

1699 - Additional French settlements would be established in Mississippi and Louisiana.

January 26, 1700 - The Cascadia earthquake, located off the coast of the Pacific Northwest along the Juan de Fuca plate, occurs. The magnitude 9 (8.7 to 9.2) quake caused a tsunami to hit the coast of Japan.

February 29, 1704 - During Queen Anne's War, Deerfield, Massachusetts is attacked by French and Indian forces with fifty-six killed and over one hundred captured and carried off.

April 24, 1704 - The first regular newspaper publishes its initial edition in Boston, the News-Letter. It was begun by John Campbell, the postmaster.

October 5, 1710 - British Troops begin a nine day siege on the French fort, Port Royal in Nova Scotia, before capturing it for the crown in the Queen-Anne's War 1701-1713.

April 6, 1712 - New York slave revolt results in six suicides and twenty-one executions.

April 11, 1713 - The Queen Anne's War ends with the French signing a treaty in the series of Treaties of Utrecht to give Nova Scotia to the British.

1716 - The first theater in the colonies opens for business in Williamsburg, Virginia.

May 7, 1718 - French colonists under the governor of the French colony of Louisiana, Jean-Baptiste le Moyne, Sieur de Bienvile, with the French Mississippi Company found the City of New Orleans, named after the regent of France, Philip II, the Duke of Orleans. It is located on the lands of the Chitimacha tribe.

November 22, 1718 - The English pirate Blackbeard is killed off the coast of Ocracoke Island in North Carolina by the crew of Lieutenant Robert Maynard of HMS.

June 16, 1720 - The Villasur expedition of Spanish troops leaves Mexico on a mission to control the increasing presence of the French in the Great Plains. It would end with a defeat by the

Pawnee on August 14 near the Loup and Platte Rivers, near Columbus, Nebraska.

1721 - Adrien de Pauger designs plans for the French Quarter in the city of New Orleans.

October 2, 1729 - Benjamin Franklin buys an interest in the Pennsylvania Gazette, founded one year earlier by Samuel Keimer.

December 28, 1732 - Poor Richard's Almanac is published for the first of its twenty-six annual editions by Benjamin Franklin in Philadelphia. It would sell as many as 10,000 copies per year.

1735 - Freedom of the Press became recognized in New York after the trial of John Peter Zenger, who had been accused of libeling the British Government in his Weekly Journal. Zenger was acquitted.

1740 - Alaska is reached by Captain Vitas Bering under the employment of the Russians.

March 18, 1741 - Twenty-nine years after the first revolt of slaves in New York, a second uprising occurs. Seventeen slaves were hanged after the revolt, thirteen burned, and seventy deported.

1741 - Thomas Faunce, the Plymouth Colony's town record keeper, identifies the exact rock that lore and stories from his father had stated was the landing rock.

June 15, 1752 - Benjamin Franklin invents the lightning rod after earlier in the year proving that lightning was electricity by flying a kite in a thunderstorm.

May 28, 1754 - George Washington and his troops attack Fort Duquesne, an initial action of the French and Indian War between the English and French which began when French forces built and occupied Fort Duquesne in Pittsburgh and did not heed warnings to leave Virginia territory.

July 25, 1755 - Decision to relocate Acadian French from Nova Scotia is made. British relocate 11,500 Acadian French to other

British colonies and France over the next eight years; some later settle in Louisiana.

November 13, 1762 - France cedes Louisiana to Spain. This started a contentious period of thirty-eight years of Spanish rule before Spain returned Louisiana back to France.

February 10, 1763 - French and Indian War ends with peace treaty that cedes Canada and the American midwest to English. This signals and effectively tightens the control of Great Britain's colonial administration of North America.

April 6, 1764 - The Sugar Act places a duty on various commodities, including lumber, food, molasses, and rum in the British colonies.

October 7, 1765 - After the establishment of the Stamp Act by the British Government, which required revenue stamps, taxes, to pay for British troops, nine American colonies hold a Stamp Act Congress in New York and adopted a Declaration of Rights against taxation without representation.

March 18, 1766 - Stamp Act is repealed.

1767 - Additional levies are put on goods in American colonies by the British Government when the Townshend Acts are enacted, including levies on glass, painter's lead, paper, and tea. All would be repealed in three years, except for the tax on tea.

July 14, 1769 - Jose de Galvez sends Spanish missionaries into California to begin the establishment of missions at San Diego and Monterey. There would be twenty-one missions established and maintained over the next sixty-four years of the mission period in Spanish California history.

1770

March 5, 1770 - Boston Massacre occurs when British troops fire into a Boston mob, who were demonstrating against British troops at the customs commission. The first to fall was Crispus Attucks, a fugitive slave and merchant seaman near the front, followed by four other men amongst the forty-fifty patriots. This event was later credited as the first battle in the American Revolution, which began five years later, and was used as an incident to further the colonists cause of rebellion.

April 12, 1770 - The Townshend Acts, duties on goods such as lead, paper, glass and tea enacted three years earlier, were repealed by British parliament, except for that on tea, thus continuing to raise opposition in America. British Prime Minister Lord North, as well as parliament, maintained the tea tax, in order to show their supremacy.

June 3, 1770 - A town of Monterey, California is established by Father Junípero Serra and explorer Gaspar de Portolà. Monterey would serve as the capital of California from 1777 to 1849 under the flags of Spain and Mexico.

July 1, 1770 - The closest encounter of a comet with earth likely occurs as the Lexell Comet passes at the closest distance in history, 3.4 million kilometers. This comet no longer comes near enough to Earth to be seen due to gravitational pulls with Jupiter and may have been ejected from our solar system.

August 1, 1770 - William Clark, explorer noted for his Lewis and Clark Expedition, and later Governor of the Missouri Territory and Superintendent of Indian Affairs, is born.

1771

The colonies are growing. By this year, there were over two hundred miles of roads in New Hampshire alone.

May 1771 - In Connecticut, the General Assembly directs the governor, Jonathan Trimball, to "collect all publick letters and papers which hereafter in any way affect the interest of this Colony and have the same bound together, that they may be preserved."

September 8, 1771 - The Mission San Gabriel in San Gabriel, California is founded by Fathers Pedro Cambon and Angel Somera, closing the gap between the established missions at Monterey and San Diego, and the new mission at San Antonio de Padua, also founded earlier in the year. Due to its large production of crops and wines, the mission later became known as the "Pride of the Missions."

November 25, 1771 - The colony of New York gains another member of the press corps when the Albany Gazette becomes that city's first newspaper into publication. It would publish until 1845.

December 31, 1771 - Imports to America from England totaled 4,200,000 pounds for the year.

1772
May 1772 - The first independent Anglo-American government is founded by the Watauga Association in East Tennessee, a group of settlers needing mutual protection along the Watauga River. The written agreement allowed for a five man court to act as the government. Also is 1772, the Wataugans would negotiate a ten year lease with the Cherokee for land along the river.

June 9, 1772 - British customs cutter HMS Gaspee, charged with enforcing the Stamp Act of 1865 and the Townshend Acts, is lured aground off the coast of Warwick, Rhode Island on the shore of Narragansett Bay. The next day, colonial sympathizers defy the king and torch the revenue ship.

November 2, 1772 - Samuel Adams organizes the Committee of Correspondence, a forerunner of the union of American colonies, that begins the American Revolution. The meeting was held in Faneuil Hall, Boston, and later repeated throughout the American colonies.

Governor Livingston, first governor of the State of New Jersey, builds Liberty Hall in Union.

November 20, 1772 - Samuel Adams writes his "Rights of the

Colonists" document, The Report of the Committee of Correspondence to the Boston Town Meeting.

1773
March 12, 1773 - The House of Burgesses in the Colony of Virginia reacts strongly against British policies by setting up a committee to contact the other colonies about their common defense. They issue the Virginia Resolutions Establishing A Committee of Correspondence.

September 11, 1773 - Benjamin Franklin writes and publishes a satirical essay in The Public Advertiser called Rules By Which A Great Empire May Be Reduced To A Small One.

November 29, 1773 - The first organized meeting of colonists in Faneuil Hall to decide what to do about the tea problem occurs after the first ship, Dartmouth, arrives at the Griffin wharf in Boston with the cargo.

December 16, 1773 - When the English East India Company sought financial assistance, England allows the company to ship surplus tea to America at low cost. This rankled the American colonists, who resented the implementation of a single company controlling the tea trade, as well as the right of the British government to tax the colonies without their consent. Meeting at the Old South Meeting House, Bostonians led by Josiah Quincy and Samuel Adams discussed the new British tax on tea and subsequently boarded three ships in the nearby harbor, tossing the 342 chests of tea overboard. The Boston Tea Party caused Parliament to close the port of Boston and pushed the American colonies one step closer to war.

The laws and ordinances of the city of Albany, New York are published.

1774
March 31, 1774 - British Parliament closes the port of Boston in response to the Boston Tea Party.

June 2, 1774 - The Intolerable Acts, including the reestablishment of the Quartering Act, requiring colonists allow British soldiers into their homes, and the curtailment of

Massachusetts self-rule, are enacted by the British government. Later led to the 3rd Amendment of the U.S. Constitution, which prohibits the U.S. Army from doing the same.

September 5 to October 26, 1774 - The First Continental Congress is held in Carpenter's Hall in Philadelphia, protesting the Intolerable Acts. The Congress, attended by all American colonies except Georgia, petitioned King George to stop the new regulations on Massachusetts, and called for civil disobedience and boycotts of British wares by the American Association. No concessions were made by the King or English parliament.

September 21, 1774 - George Mason and George Washington form the Fairfax County Militia Association, which is independent of British control. It would consist of no more than one hundred men.

The colonies of Rhode Island, Georgia, and Connecticut ban the further importation of slaves.

1775
By the end of January 1775, there were 37 newspapers being printed in the American colonies. Seven newspapers were published in Massachusetts; one in New Hampshire; two in Rhode Island; and 4 in Connecticut. Three papers were published in New York City, with one additional New York paper published in Albany. Nine were published in Pennsylvania; two in Maryland; two in Virginia (both at Williamsburg); two in North Carolina; three in South Carolina, and one in Georgia.

February 9, 1775 - The British government declares Massachusetts in rebellion.

March 23, 1775 - Patrick Henry addresses the Virginia House of Burgesses in St. John's Church in Richmond, where he decreed, "Give me Liberty or Give me Death." His speech is often credited with convincing Virginia to permit Virginia troops to enter the Revolutionary War. The crowd reacted to Henry's speech with fervent cries, "To Arms! To Arms!"

April 18, 1775 - Two lanterns were hung from the steeple of Old North Church by sexton Robert Newman as Paul Revere and

William Dawes rode through the night, warning patriots that the British were coming to Concord to destroy arms. The next day, during armed resistance, 8 Minutemen were killed at Lexington and the British took 273 casualties on their return from Concord, starting the American Revolution. This was a culmination of the months prior, as colonists began to gather arms and powder if fighting the British became necessary. However, even after the patriot's brave battle at Lexington and Concord, the majority of Americans were undecided whether war or reconciliation was the more prudent course of action.

June 15, 1775 - The Continental Congress appoints George Washington commander-in-chief of the Continental Army, sending him to Boston with the task to take charge of the ragtag militia there.

1776
January 10, 1776 - Thomas Paine, an English writer, publishes his pamphlet "Common Sense," touting the ability and right of America to create a democratic and free nation, winning public support for the cause of American independence from Britain with the sale of hundreds of thousands of copies. Thomas Jefferson received a copy of "Common Sense" at his home Monticello, whose sentiments pleased him, and the course for independence and the Declaration to follow began.

July 4, 1776 - The Declaration of Independence, from the pen of Thomas Jefferson and his committee, is approved in the Second Continental Congress of the United States of America, held in Independence Hall, Philadelphia, Pennsylvania. It was influenced by many writers, including John Locke, and was emboldened by the notion that man had the natural right to change or overthrow the government that denied their rights. Four days later, the Declaration of Independence was proclaimed publicly for the first time outside the Province House in Philadelphia, later to be dubbed Independence Hall, touching off a celebration that rippled through the city. Liberty and freedom was celebrated amongst commoners and soldiers, who would soon fight to solidify its hold on the thirteen colonies.

September 7, 1776 - In the world's first submarine attack, the American submersible ship Turtle attempts to attach a time bomb to the flagship of British Admiral Richard Howe's ship HMS Eagle in New York Harbor.

September 22, 1776 - As a member of the Continental Army sent on an intelligence gathering mission behind enemy lines on Long Island, Nathan Hale, disguised as a Dutch teacher, is subsequently caught and executed by the British for spying. In a speech before he was hung, the immortal words, "I only regret that I have but one life to lose for my country," were reportedly uttered, and reverberated through repetition throughout the colonies. A statue of Hale now sits outside the Central Intelligence Agency in Washington, D.C.

December 25 to 26, 1776 - At McKonkey's Ferry, General Washington and his 2,400 troops cross the Delaware River from Pennsylvania to New Jersey on Christmas Day from 4 p.m. until 4 a.m. the next morning and defeats 1,400 Hessians in the 1st Battle of Trenton, capturing 900 men.

1777

January 3, 1777 - General Washington and the 7,000 man Continental Army defeats British General Charles Cornwallis at Princeton, New Jersey. This battle, combined with that of Trenton one week earlier, impressed upon other European nations that the Americans could combat the British Army.

June 14, 1777 - The Continental Congress adopts the Stars and Stripes as the national flag. It would later fly on the battlefield for the first time on September 3rd at Cooch's Bridge, Delaware.

August 3, 1777 - American held Fort Stanwix is besieged by British and Indian troops under the command of General Barry St. Leger. The British are forced to withdraw after three weeks under the duress of the fort's defenders, led by Colonel Peter Gansevoort.

November 15, 1777 - The Articles of Confederation and Perpetual Union are adopted by the Continental Congress in Independence Hall. It serves as the first constitution of the United States.

December 17, 1777 - After John Adams, elected commissioner

to France by the Continental Congress, and Benjamin Franklin engage their support for the Revolutionary War, France recognizes the independence of the 13 colonies, signing treaties of alliance and commerce. French involvement becomes the turning point of the war.

December 19, 1777 - After failing victory in the battles of Brandywine and Germantown, and in response to the British capture of Philadelphia, George Washington marches his 11,000 man Continental Army into Valley Forge for the first winter encampment.

1778
In an advertisement in a Kentucky gazette, a New Jersey stallion gains the name thoroughbred, the first usage in the United States of that equine term.

February 5, 1778 - Friedrich von Steuben of the Prussian Army meets with the Continental Congress in York, Pennsylvania. They direct him to join General George Washington at the winter encampment at Valley Forge to drill the Continental Army into an effective fighting unit while the British retain control of Philadelphia, only twenty miles away. South Carolina also becomes the first state to ratify the Articles of Confederation.

February 6, 1778 - France signs the treaty of Amity and Commerce with the United States, officially recognizing the new nation, and sends Pierre L'Enfant to be captain of engineers at Valley Forge. Later, L'Enfant would be commissioned to design the capital city of the United States, Washington, D.C.

June 18, 1778 - British evacuate Philadelphia to reinforce their troops in New York City, a response to the new French involvement in the conflict.

December 29, 1778 - The first battle of Savannah, Georgia is lost to the British.

1779
February 25, 1779 - Fort Sackville at Vincennes, Indiana is surrendered by British troops under the command of British Lt. Governor Henry Hamilton. The militia under Lt. Colonel George

Rogers Clark, bolsters the western claims in the American Revolution.

June 1, 1779 - Although currently a successful American general, Benedict Arnold is court-marshaled for civil authority disputes. His sentence, however, was a light reprimand by General Washington. Mad about the court-marshal and the new American alliance with France, Arnold became a traitor against the American cause when he plotted to transfer the fort at West Point, New York, for 20,000 sterling (approximately $1,000,000 today) that would effectively give control of the Hudson River to British forces. His plot was uncovered, but Arnold escaped, then joined British forces and fought against the Continental Army.

September 23, 1779 - John Paul Jones and the Bonhomme Richard defeat the Serapis in the British North Sea.

December 1, 1779 - General Washington arrives at Morristown, New Jersey, where the Continental Army winters in the second season of the Revolutionary War.

December 25, 1779 - Nashville, Tennessee is founded by James Robertson as Fort Nashborough.

1780
May 12, 1780 - Charleston, South Carolina falls to the British after an effective siege.

Prompted by poor vision both near and far, and tired of putting his glasses on and off, Benjamin Franklin invents bi-focals. It is unknown exactly when this occurred, with Franklin admitting to friends that he had been wearing double spectacles in 1784.

July 11, 1780 - French troops set foot on American soil at Newport, Rhode Island, to fight alongside the Patriot militiamen of the Continental Army for American independence from Great Britain.

September 25, 1780 - The march begins this date at Sycamore Shoals on the Watauga River (Tennessee) by the "over-mountain men" militia of the American Revolution under Colonels James McDowell, John Sevier, Isaac Shelby, and William Campbell as they move toward the Battle of Kings Mountain in South Carolina.

October 7, 1780 - Loyalist troops fighting for Britain are beaten at the Battle of Kings Mountain by the "over-mountain men," who kill the opposition leader British Major General Patrick Ferguson. This battle reversed the southern fortunes of the British during the Revolutionary War.

1781
January 17, 1781 - At Cowpens, South Carolina, Brigadier General Daniel Morgan with his band of Patriot militia defeat the large force of British regulars under Lt. Colonel Banastre Tarleton. This engagement in the southern sphere of the American Revolution provided a key victory for American forces.

March 15, 1781 - British troops under Lord Cornwallis gain a costly victory at the Battle of Guilford Courthouse in North Carolina at the expense of Major General Nathanael Greene in the opening salvo of the campaign that would lead to Yorktown.

May 22, 1781 - Major General Nathanael Greene and Harry "Light-horse" Lee leads the Continental Army against British loyalists in a siege at Ninety-Six, South Carolina. They are repulsed and forced to withdraw on June 18 when Colonel John Cruger leads British loyalists to victory against an attack of the Continental Army.

May 26, 1781 - The Bank of North America is incorporated in Philadelphia by an act of Congress to help stabilize the issuance of paper currency. It was capitalized in 1781 with $400,000.

September 26, 1781 - General George Washington and Rochambeau join forces near Williamsburg. Two weeks later, on October 6, they begin the siege of Cornwall at Yorktown. At the time, English troops numbered 6,000, American troops 8,846, and French troops 7,800. On October 19, British forces under Lord Cornwall surrender to Washington's American forces and their French allies at Yorktown, Virginia. This would be the last military battle of the American Revolution.

1782
January 4, 1782 - The Bank of North America opens its doors as Robert Morris, the superintendent of Finance, recommends the creation of a national mint and decimal coins. The bank, along with the Bank of New York and First Bank of the United States, will be the first entities to obtain shares on the New York Stock Exchange.

March 20, 1782 - Lord North resigns as British Prime Minister, leading the way for a New British cabinet to agree to recognize United States independence.

June 20, 1782 - The Bald Eagle is adopted by Congress as the national bird.

July 11, 1782 - British troops begin to leave United States' soil, evacuating Savannah, Georgia. On December 14, they would continue their evacuation by leaving Charleston, South Carolina.

November 7, 1782 - British Parliament agrees to the recognition of U.S. independence. A preliminary peace treaty, later formalized as the "Treaty of Paris" is signed between American and British officials in Paris on November 30.

1783

April 15, 1783 - Congress ratifies the preliminary peace treaty, ending the Revolutionary War.

April 1783 - Massachusetts Supreme Court outlaws slavery, citing the state Bill of Rights "all men are born free and equal."

September 3, 1783 - In Paris, France, John Adams leads an American delegation and signs the peace treaty officially ending the Revolutionary War between the United States and Britain.

November 3, 1783 - The Continental Army is ordered disbanded by General George Washington. After the British leave New York City on November 25, Washington bids goodbye to his officers at Fraunces Tavern in New York City on December 4.

Noah Webster publishes the American Spelling Book, a bestseller. More than a million copies are sold of "Webster's Dictionary." Webster's Dictionary is credited for standardizing spelling and pronunciation in the United States of America.

1784

January 14, 1784 - Congress ratifies the final peace treaty between Great Britain and the United States, ending the conflict that would give America its freedom.

March 1, 1784 - All children born after this date in 1784 in Rhode Island are free. Rhode Island's passage of its Emancipation Act provided for the gradual abolishment of the right to hold slaves.

September 21, 1784 - The Pennsylvania Packet General Advertiser is published, the first successful daily newspaper in the United States.

By the end of 1784, trade with Great Britain had returned as Britain receives its first bales of imported American cotton.

November 24, 1784 - Zachary Taylor, who would become the 12th president of the United States, is born.

1785

January 7, 1785 - Dr. John Jeffries, an American physician, joins

John-Pierre Blanchard, a French aviation pioneer, to become the first men to cross the English channel by air, traveling from Dover, England to Calais, France in a hydrogen gas balloon.

June 3, 1785 - The Continental Navy is disbanded.

July 6, 1785 - The United States adopts a decimal coinage system, with the dollar overwhelmingly selected as the monetary unit, the first time any nation has done so.

August 23, 1785 - Oliver Hazard Perry, American naval officer, is born.

Stewart Dean, the most famous navigator of Albany, New York, sails from Albany to China from late 1784 through the year of 1785. Dean, on the private schooner Nimrod, had been captured by the British at St. Kitts in 1782, and later released.

1786
January 3, 1786 - The Third Treaty of Hopewell is signed between representatives of the Confederation Congress of the United States and the Indian nation of the Choctaw, originally located in the southeastern states of Mississippi, Alabama, and Louisiana and known as one of the five civilized tribes.

August 17, 1786 - American frontiersman David "Davy" Crockett is born.

September 11-14, 1786 - Five state delegates at a meeting in Annapolis, Maryland call for Congress to hold a convention in Philadelphia in order to write a constitution for the thirteen states.

December 1786 - Columbian magazine publishes sketch of John Fitch's new invention, the steamboat. He launches it on the Delaware River in 1787 with six large paddles, like an Indian canoe, that was powered by a steam engine.

Rhode Island farmers strike against merchants who refused to accept the depreciated paper currency.

1787
January 25, 1787 - In Massachusetts, six hundred debt-ridden

farmers, led by Daniel Shays, revolt against their creditors and high Massachusetts taxes. Faced with imprisonment and the loss of their farms for not paying their debts, they engage in Shays' Rebellion, but it fails when state militia intervene. Daniel Shays would escape to Vermont with the death penalty on his head, but later would be pardoned for his actions.

May 25, 1787 - With George Washington presiding, the Constitutional Convention opens in Philadelphia's Independence Hall.

July 5, 1787 - A compromise during the Constitutional Convention proposed by Roger Sherman of Connecticut solves the problem of the amount of votes each state would receive in Congress. A bicameral legislature would be enacted, with equal votes for the Senate and proportional representation based on population in the House of Representatives.

July 13, 1787 - The Northwest Ordinance, which determined a government for the Northwest Territory of the United States (north of the Ohio River and west of New York), is adopted by the Continental Congress. It guaranteed freedom of religion, school support, and no slavery, plus the opportunity for statehood.

September 17, 1787 - Delegates to the Constitutional Convention adopt the Constitution.

1788
January 2, 1788 - States of the United States continue to ratify the U.S. Constitution when Georgia becomes the 4th state to do so.

January 22, 1788 - Cyrus Griffin is elected as the last president of the Continental Congress prior to official ratification of the United States Constitution.

March 21, 1788 - Twenty-five percent of the population of New Orleans perish in a tragic fire that destroyed 856 buildings and left the majority of the city in ruins.

June 21, 1788 - Ratification by New Hampshire of the United States Constitution, the 9th state to do so, indicates adoption of the document by the United States.

October 24, 1788 - Sarah Josepha Hale, American author of the nursery rhyme, "Mary Had a Little Lamb," and her campaign to officially recognize Thanksgiving as a holiday, is born.

1789
February 4, 1789 - The 1st Congress meets in Federal Hall, New York City with regular sessions beginning two months later on April 6. Frederick A. Muhlenberg becomes the first Speaker of the newly formed House of Representatives. George Washington is elected unanimously by the Electoral College as the 1st President of the United States.

March 4, 1789 - In Federal Hall, New York City, a converted Customs House, the government of the United States under the United States Constitution begins to act. The U.S. Constitution is declared to be in effect.

April 30, 1789 - The 1st President, George Washington, is inaugurated in New York City. He had been chosen president by all voting electors (there was no direct presidential election) with John Adams elected Vice President.

September 24, 1789 - The Federal Judiciary Act is passed, creating the Supreme Court.

September 25, 1789 - The Bill of Rights is submitted to the states by Congress.

1790
January 8, 1790 - The first State of the Union address is given by first president George Washington.

February 1, 1790 - The Supreme Court of the United States convenes for the initial session.

March 1, 1790 - Congress commissions the first U.S. census. When completed, it shows that 3,929,214 lived in the nascent democracy in 1790. The most populated state, Virginia, has 691,737. The center of population was 23 miles west of Baltimore, Maryland.

July 16, 1790 - George Washington, as President, approves the Residence Bill, legislation that authorizes the buying of land along the Potomac River for federal buildings and parks, creating the District of Columbia.

July 31, 1790 - The first patent in the United States is issued to inventor Samuel Hopkins for improved method of making potash.

1791
March 3, 1791 - The United States Congress passes a resolution to establish the U.S. Mint, which is created one year later when the Coinage Act is passed on April 2.

March 14, 1791 - Vermont is added as the 14th State. Carved from portions of New York and New Hampshire, and first known as New Connecticut, Vermont spent fourteen years as an independent republic before joining the Union.

April 27, 1791 - Samuel Morse, United State inventor, is born. He would later develop the Morse code for use in the first electric telegraph in the United States.

August 26, 1791 - The steamboat is patented in the United States by John Fitch. First launched on the Delaware River in 1787, and operated passenger service from Philadelphia to Burlington, New Jersey, which proved unprofitable.

December 15, 1791 - In Philadelphia's Congress Hall, the Bill of Rights, which constitutes the first ten amendments to the Constitution, takes effect. Two of the original twelve amendments do not pass.

1792
February 20, 1792 - The United States Post Office Department is established, signed into law by President George Washington.

April 5, 1792 - The presidential veto is used for the first time when President Washington turns down a bill to apportion representation amongst the states.

May 17, 1792 - The beginnings of the New York Stock Exchange is established with the signing of the Buttonwood agreement.

October 13, 1792 - The cornerstone for the U.S. Executive Mansion (called the White House since 1818) in the new District of Columbia is laid by freemasons and the commissioners of the district during the construction of the home of the president. It would take eight more years before President John Adams would move into the home.

December 3, 1792 - George Washington, a Federalist, is reelected president of the United States with no opposition, with John Adams elected Vice President. The Federalists, who believed in a strong central government, outnumbered the other political party at the time, the Democrat-Republicans, who decided against a political fight due to Washington's popularity. Washington had considered not seeking a second term, but decided to serve again, in some part due to trying to stem the tide of political parties.

1793
February 12, 1793 - The United States Congress passes a federal law requiring the return of slaves that escaped from slave states into free territory or states.

April 22, 1793 - George Washington signs the Proclamation of Neutrality in the French Revolutionary Wars, where France has already declared war on England, the Netherlands, Austria, Prussia, and Sardinla.

August 17, 1793 - Dr. Benjamin Rush confers with two Philadelphia doctors about an epidemic of disease along the docks of Philadelphia over the preceding two weeks. By November, over 10% of the population of the city had succumbed, nearly 5,000 people. The disease had been brought to the city by refugees from Haiti, then coupled with a wet spring and swamps that became an incubator for mosquitos.

September 18, 1793 - George Washington lays the cornerstone in the Capitol building, beginning the construction on the design by Dr. William Thornton.

December 9, 1793 - The American Minerva, established by Noah Webster, becomes New York City's first daily newspaper.

1794
March 14, 1794 - Eli Whitney patents the cotton gin, which could do the work of fifty men when cleaning cotton by hand.

March 27, 1794 - The U.S. Government establishes a permanent navy and commissions six vessels to be built. They would be put into service three years later.

August 20, 1794 - General Anthony Wayne, commander of the Ohio-Indiana area, routs a confederacy of Indian tribes, including Shawnee, Mingo, Delaware, Wyandot, Miami, Ottawa, Chippewa, and Potawatomi, at Fallen Timbers on the Maumee River, causing a retreat in disarray.

September 1, 1794 - The Whiskey Rebellion occurs when western Pennsylvania farmers in the Monongahela Valley, upset over the liquor tax passed in 1791, are suppressed by 15,000 militia sent by Alexander Hamilton to establish the authority of the federal government to uphold its laws.

November 19, 1794 - Jay's Treaty is signed between the United States of America and the Kingdom of Great Britain. This treaty tried to settle some of the lingering troubles stemming from the American Revolution.

1795
January 14, 1795 - The University of North Carolina, at Chapel

Hill, becomes the first operating state university in the United States, and the only public university to graduate students in the 18th century.

February 7, 1795 - The United States passes the 11th amendment to the U.S. Constitution on the subject of each state's sovereign immunity.

August 3, 1795 - General Wayne signs a peace treaty with the Indians at Fort Greenville, Ohio, ending the hostilities in what was then known as the Northwest Territories after the Indian confederation's defeat (the treaty included the above mentioned tribes, as well as the Eel Rivers, Weas, Kickapoos, Piankeshaws, and Kaskaskias) at Fallen Timbers the year before.

October 27, 1795 - The Treaty of Madrid is signed, establishing the boundaries between the Spanish Colonies and the United States.

November 28, 1795 - The United States purchases peace with Tunis and Algiers by supplying a frigate and over $800,000.

1796
June 1, 1796- Tennessee is admitted into the Union as the 16th state.

July 11, 1796 - Possession of the city of Detroit by the United States is taken by terms of the Jay Treaty with Great Britain.

September 19, 1796 - President George Washington gives his final address as president, published in the American Daily Advertiser, urging strong warnings against permanent foreign alliances, large public debt, and a large military establishment.

November 4 to December 7, 1796 - The U.S. Electoral College meets to elect Federalist John Adams as president. John Adams defeated Thomas Jefferson, of the Democrat Republican party, whose platform included the notion of a weak central government, in the U.S. presidential election. Political parties came into prominence with this election after the retirement of George Washington. Electors who chose the president were chosen by the states, using various methods, including the popular vote or by state legislators. Adams received 71 electoral votes to Jefferson's 68.

1797
January 3, 1797 - The Treaty of Tripoli, signifying peace between the United States and Tripoli, is signed at Algiers.

March 4, 1797 - John Adams succeeds George Washington as president of the United States.

July 10, 1797 - The first of three ships, the U.S. frigate United States, is launched by the United States on this day as it begins to build up its navy. Later in 1797, the other two ships would be launched; the Constellation in Baltimore on September 7; and the Constitution (old Ironsides) in Boston, September 20.

October 21, 1797 - The Constitution, a 44 gun frigate, is sent into service from Boston Harbor against Barbary pirates off the coast of Tripoli.

December 17, 1797 - Joseph Henry, an American scientist is born. He would serve as the first president of the Smithsonian Institution and is credited with discoveries in the field of electro magnets.

1798
May 4, 1798 - Thomas Jefferson, then Vice President of the United States, informs the American Philosophical Society of his invention of a new mould board for a plow.

April 7, 1798 - The Territory of Mississippi is established from parts of Georgia and South Carolina, and later expanded to include disputed territory of the United States and Spain.

German-American Gottlieb Graupner settles in Boston and becomes the father of orchestral music in the United States. He would later organize the Philharmonic Society.

July 7, 1798 - Congress voids all treaties with France due to French raids on U.S. ships and a rejection of its diplomats, and orders the Navy to capture French armed ships. Eight-four

French ships are captured by the U.S. Navy (with 45 ships) and private ships (365).

July 14, 1798 - The Alien and Sedition Acts making it a federal crime to publish malicious statements about the United States Government go into law.

1799
February 9, 1799 - The French warship L'Insurgente is captured by the U.S.S. Constellation. Napoleon stops the French raids after becoming First Consul.

February 15, 1799 - The first printed ballots in the United States are printed in Pennsylvania.

March 29, 1799 - A law is passed to abolish slavery in the state of New York, effective twenty-eight years later, in 1827.

The American System of Manufacturing is invented by Eli Whitney, who uses semi-skilled labor, machine tools, and jigs to make standardized, interchangeable parts, then an assembly line of labor. Whitney first used the system to manufacture 10,000 muskets for the U.S. Government.

December 14, 1799 - George Washington, the 1st commander of the Revolution and President of the United States, passes at his estate in Virginia.

1800
April 23, 1800 - The Natchez Trace post route, following an old trail running from Nashville, Tennessee to Natchez, Mississippi, is established by an Act of Congress.

April 24, 1800 - The United States Library of Congress is founded.

August 4, 1800 - The second census of the United States is conducted. The total population of the USA was 5,308,483 and the center of its population was 18 miles west of Baltimore, Maryland.

November 1, 1800 - U.S. President John Adams is the first President to live in the White House, then known as the Executive Mansion and sixteen days later, the United States Congress holds its first session in Washington, D.C. He would be defeated for the presidency by December 6 by Thomas Jefferson.

Slavery is ended in the Northwest Territory, stemming from the Ordinance of 1787 establishing the territory and written by Thomas Jefferson. Jefferson had proposed that all slavery be prohibited by the year 1800, but that proposal had been defeated by one vote.

1801
January 20, 1801 - John Marshall is appointed Chief Justice of the Supreme Court of the United States.

February 17, 1801 - Thomas Jefferson is elected as the 3rd president of the United States in a vote of the House of Representatives after tying Aaron Burr, his Vice President, in the electoral college with 73 electors due to a flaw in the original vote for two system, which would be corrected in the 12th Amendment to the Constitution.

March 4, 1801 - Thomas Jefferson is inaugurated for his first term as President of the United States.

May 10, 1801 - Tripoli declares war against the United States. The United States had refused to pay additional tribute to commerce raiding corsairs from Arabia.

November 16, 1801 - The first edition of the New York Post is published.

1802
February 11, 1802 - Lydia Child is born and would become a foremost author expounding the idea of an American abolitionist.

March 16, 1802 - West Point, New York is established. Four months later, the United States Military Academy opens on July 4.

May 22, 1802 - Martha Washington, the first First Lady of the United States, passes.

October 2, 1802 - War ends between Tripoli and Sweden, but continues with the United States, despite a negotiated peace, due to compensation disagreements.

December 15, 1802 - Thomas Jefferson gives his Second State of the Nation address to the House and Senate, focusing on peace in the European conflict and payment of the public debt.

1803
January 30, 1803 - Discussions to buy New Orleans begin when Monroe and Livingston sail to Paris, ending with the complete purchase of the Louisiana Purchase three months later.

February 24, 1803 - The United States Supreme Court overturns its first U.S. law in the case of Marbury versus Madison, establishing the context of judicial review as they declared a statute within the Constitution void. This established the Supreme Court's position as an equal member of the three branches of United States government.

March 1, 1803 - Ohio is admitted to the Union as the 17th U.S. state.

April 30, 1803 - President Thomas Jefferson doubles the size of the United States of America with his purchase of the Louisiana Territory from Napoleon's France, thus paving way for the western expansion that would mark the entire history of the 19th century from Missouri to the Pacific Coast. The price of the purchase included bonds of $11,250,000 and $3,750,000 in payments to United States citizens with claims against France.

December 20, 1803 - The United States of America takes title to the Louisiana Purchase, which stretches the United States from the Canadian border to the mouth of the Mississippi River.

1804
February 15, 1804 - New Jersey becomes the last northern state to abolish slavery.

May 14, 1804 - Ordered by Thomas Jefferson to map the Northwest United States, Lewis and Clark begin their expedition from St. Louis and Camp Dubois. The journey begins with navigation of the Missouri River.

July 11, 1804 - The duel between Alexander Hamilton and Vice President Aaron Burr, longtime political rivals, occurs in Weehawken, New Jersey, culminating in the death of Hamilton.

October 1, 1804 - The attack on Sitka, Alaska by Russians and their allies in the Aleut community siege a Tlingit Indian fort. One week later, the siege was complete with the driving out of Tlingit forces.

October 26, 1804 - The Lewis and Clark Expedition arrives at the confluence of the Knife and Missouri Rivers, in what is now the state of North Dakota, where they camped until the spring of 1805 at the hospitality of the Mandan and Minitari Indian villages.

November 4 to December 5, 1804 - Thomas Jefferson wins reelection over Charles Pinckney with 162 to 14 Electoral College votes.

1805
January 11, 1805 - The Michigan Territory is established.

April 27, 1805 - American Marines and Berbers attack the Tripoli city of Derna. Land and naval forces would battle against Tripoli until peace was concluded with the United States on June 4, 1805.

June 13, 1805 - Meriweather Lewis and four companions confirm their correct heading by sighting the Great Falls of the Missouri River, as the Lewis and Clark expedition continues west.

December 8, 1805 - Members of the Lewis and Clark expedition upon sighting the Pacific Ocean on November 15, build Fort Clatsop, a log fort near the mouth of the Columbia River in present-day Oregon. They would spend the winter of 1805-1806 in the newly constructed fort.

December 23, 1805 - The founder of Mormonism, Joseph Smith, Jr. is born.

1806
March 23, 1806 - Explorers Lewis and Clark and the Corps of Discovery begin the several thousand mile trek back to St. Louis, Missouri from their winter camp near the Pacific Ocean.

March 29, 1806 - The National Road, also known as the Great National Pike or the Cumberland Road, the first federally funded highway that ran between Cumberland, Maryland to Ohio, is approved by President Thomas Jefferson with the signing of legislation and appropriation of $30,000. The highway ran through three states; Maryland, Pennsylvania, and Ohio.

July 15, 1806 - A second exploratory expedition led by U.S. Army Lieutenant Zebulon Pike begins from Fort Bellefountaine near St. Louis. Later that year, during a second trip, he reaches the distant Colorado foothills of the Rocky Mountains and discovers Pike's Peak.

September 23, 1806 - The Lewis and Clark Expedition to map the northwest United States ends. Essential to the journey was Sacagawea, their female Indian guide.

Noah Webster publishes his first American English dictionary.

1807
January 19, 1807 - Robert E. Lee is born. Would become a military officer, both with the U.S. Regular Army prior to the outbreak of Civil War, and afterwards, the American Confederate General.

February 17, 1807 - Vice President Aaron Burr is arrested for treason in Alabama, charged with a scheme to annex parts of Louisiana and Mexico into an independent republic. Three months later, a grand jury indicts the former Vice President under the same charges.

March 2, 1807 - Congress passes an act that prohibits the importation of slaves into any port within the confines of the United States from any foreign land. It was to take effect on the 1st of January 1808.

August 17, 1807 - The first practical steamboat journey was made by Robert Fulton in the steamboat Clermont, who navigated the Hudson River from New York City to Albany in thirty-two hours, a trip of 150 miles. This becomes the first commercial steamboat service in the world.

September 1, 1807 - Aaron Burr is acquitted of treason.

1808
January 1, 1808 - The importation of slaves is outlawed, although between 1808 and 1860, more than 250,000 slaves were illegally imported.

February 11, 1808 - Anthracite coal is first burned, in an experiment, as fuel.

April 6, 1808 - The American Fur Company is incorporated by John Jacob Astor.

November 4 to December 7, 1808 - James Madison is elected as the 4th President of the United States, defeating Charles C. Pinckney.

December 29, 1808 - Andrew Johnson, the 17th President of the United States, is born in Raleigh, North Carolina to porter and church sexton Jacob Johnson and Mary McDonough. He would succeed Abraham Lincoln as president after his assassination and later be impeached for his role in removing Secretary of War Edwin M. Stanton. Johnson would be acquitted by one vote.

1809
February 3, 1809 - The Illinois Territory is created.

February 12, 1809 - Abraham Lincoln, the 16th President of the United States, is born in a humble Hardin County, Kentucky log cabin to carpenter Thomas Lincoln and Nancy Hanks.

February 20, 1809 - The Supreme Court of the United States rules that the power of the Federal Government is greater than the power of any individual state.

March 4, 1809 - James Madison is inaugurated, succeeding Thomas Jefferson as President of the United States.

August 1809 - The U.S.S. Constitution is re-commissioned as the flagship of the North Atlantic Squadron.

1810
June 23, 1810 - The Pacific Fur Company is formed by John Jacob Astor.

During 1810, the causes of the War of 1812 began to emerge. Four thousand naturalized American sailors had been seized by British forces by this year, which forced trade between England and the United States to grind to a halt.

September 8, 1810 - Thirty-three employees of the Pacific Fur Company founded by John Jacob Astor embark on a six month journey around South America from New York Harbor. Arriving at the mouth of the Columbia River on the ship Tonquin, in present day Oregon, they found the fur-trading town of Astoria.

December 3, 1810 - Ex-slave Tom Molineaux, born at a Virginia plantation in 1784, fought English boxing champion Tom Cribb, narrowly defeated after 39 rounds when he collapsed from exhaustion. A rematch was held on September 28, 1811 with Cribb retaining his title in 11 rounds.

August 6, 1810 - The center of the population of the United States, listed as 7,239,881 in the 1810 census, was only 40 miles northwest of Washington, D.C. in the state of Virginia.

1811
February 3, 1811 - American journalist, editor, and publisher, Horace Greeley, is born.

May 8, 1811 - The contract for construction of the Cumberland Road is assigned. The road, an important route through the Allegheny Mountains for westward expansion, was begun five years after authorization as the first federal highway by Thomas Jefferson in 1806. It broadly followed Braddock's Road, a military route used by George Washington in 1754. The National Road, as it would later be called, and now known as Rt. 40, measured 128 miles from Cumberland, Maryland to Wheeling, West Virginia, and would later have its terminus in Vandalia, Illinois.

October 11, 1811 - The first steam-powered ferry service between New York City and Hoboken, New Jersey is started on John Steven's ship, the Juliana.

November 7, 1811 - At the battle of Tippecanoe, Indian warriors under the command of Tecumseh and his brother Tenskwatawa, known as the Prophet, are defeated by William Henry Harrison, the governor of Indiana.

December 16, 1811 - An earthquake near New Madrid, in the Mississippi Valley, reverses the course of the Mississippi River for a period of time. This quake was the first of two major earthquakes which preceded the largest quake ever in the United States two months later.

1812
February 7, 1812 - With an estimated magnitude of 7.4 to 8.3, the final New Madrid earthquake strikes near New Madrid, Missouri. This quake was the largest earthquake ever recorded in the continental United States, destroying one-half of the town of New Madrid. It was felt strongly for 50,000 square miles, created new lakes, caused numerous aftershocks, and reversed the course of the Mississippi River. A request by William Clark, the Missouri territory governor, for federal help, actually one month earlier after the first quake recorded, may have been the first request for disaster relief.

June 1, 1812 - U.S. President James Madison asks Congress to declare war on the United Kingdom. Before the vote could be approved, on June 16, British ships raise a blockade against the United States.

June 18, 1812 - Although unaware of the blockade at the time of their vote, Madison signs declaration after Congress narrowly approves war with Great Britain. Western states generally favored the action while New England states disapproved. This included the state of Rhode Island, which would refuse to participate in the War of 1812.

August 13, 1812 - August naval battles in the War of 1812 begin with the United States Navy defeating the British when the U.S.S. Essex captured Alert. Three days later, the tide would turn in

British favor as English forces capture Fort Detroit without a fight. This would be followed up on August 19 when the U.S.S. Constitution secured another victory for the Navy of the United States off the coast of Nova Scotia when it destroyed the British frigate Guerriere, earning the nickname "Old Ironsides" when British shot bounded off the Constitution's side. On October 25, off the Azores, the U.S.S. United States defeated the Macedonian, towing the ship back to the U.S., the first British warship brought back to an American port.

October 30 to December 2, 1812 - President James Madison defeats De Witt Clinton in the U.S. presidential election, securing a second term as the United States engages in the War of 1812 by an Electoral College margin of 128 votes to 89.

1813
April 27, 1813 - The Battle of York (Toronto, Canada) is held when American troops raid and destroy, but do not occupy the city.

June 1, 1813 - The city directory of Albany, New York is first published.

June 6, 1812 - Despite having a force three times the size of its British foe, Americans lose the Battle of Stoney Creek to a British army of 700 men under John Vincent.

September 10, 1813 - The Battle of Lake Erie is won by the American navy when Commodore Perry's fleet defeats the ships of British Captain Robert Barclay. This victory allows U.S. forces to take control of the majority of the Old Northwest and lake region.

October 5, 1813 - A United States victory at the Battle of Thames, Ontario allows American forces to break the Indian allies of the English and secure the frontier of Detroit. Native Indian leader Tecumseh of the Shawnee tribe is killed during this battle.

1814

March 27, 1814 - Settlement opens in large parts of Alabama and Georgia after Andrew Jackson's militia from Tennessee defeat the Red Stick Creeks of Chief Menawa along the Tallapoosa River at Horseshoe Bend.

August 24, 1814 - The White House is burned by British forces upon the occupation of Washington, D.C. during the War of 1812. This act, in retaliation for the destruction by U.S. troops of Canadian public buildings, causes President Madison to evacuate. The British advance would be halted by Maryland militia three weeks later on September 12. Another United States president, James Monroe, would have to wait three years before he could reoccupy the executive mansion.

September 11, 1814 - The Battle of Lake Champlain is won by U.S. naval forces with the U.S.S. Ticonderoga leading the way.

September 13-14, 1814 - Francis Scott Key writes the words to the Star Spangled Banner during the twenty-five hour bombardment of Fort McHenry at the head of the river leading to the Baltimore harbor.

December 24, 1814 - A peace treaty is signed between the British and American government at Ghent, bringing to an end the War of 1812.

1815

January 8, 1815 - On the Chalmette plantation at New Orleans, five thousand three hundred British troops still unaware of the peace treaty signed two weeks earlier, attack American forces in the last battle of the War of 1812. Major General Andrew Jackson leads his American soldiers to victory over British troops under the command of Sir Edward Pakenham. British troops take over two thousand casualties; American forces seventy-one.

February 6, 1815 - The first American railroad charter is granted by the state of New Jersey to John Stephens.

August 6, 1815 - Piracy on the high seas by Algiers, Tunis, and Tripoli is effectively ended by a flotilla from the United States.

November 12, 1815 - American women's rights activist Elizabeth Cady Stanton in born.

December 25, 1815 - The oldest continuing performance arts organization in the United States, the Handel and Haydn Society of Boston, gives its first performance.

1816
April 10, 1816 - Second Bank of the United States is chartered, five years after the expiration of the 1st Bank of the United States.

Caused by the Mount Tambora volcano erupting on April 10, 1815, the entire "Year without a Summer" occurs in the northern hemisphere due to global cooling.

August 1816 - E. Remington and Sons is founded in 1816.

November 1 to December 4, 1816 - James Monroe defeats Rufus King in the United States presidential election, garnering 183 Electoral College votes to 34 for the Federalist King.

December 11, 1816 - The territory of Indiana is admitted into the United States of America as the 19th state.

1817
March 4, 1817 - James Monroe is inaugurated as the President of the United States, succeeding James Madison. His vice president, Daniel D. Tompkins, who would serve alongside Monroe for his entire eight years, was also inaugurated.

April 28-29, 1817 - The Rush-Bagot treaty is signed. This would limit the amount of armaments allowed on the Great Lakes by British and American forces.

July 4, 1817 - The construction of the Erie Canal begins at Rome, New York. The first section between Rome and Utica would be completed two years later. The canal would eventually connect the Atlantic Ocean, through the Hudson River, to the Great Lakes, with 83 locks over its 363 miles. The canal, when completed in 1825, would cut transport costs by 90%.

December 10, 1817 - The United States of America admits its 20th state, Mississippi.

The second wave of Amish immigration to North America begins in 1817, bringing 3,000 Amish from Europe to relocate in the United States. The first wave of Amish immigration occurred through 1770.

1818
March 15, 1818 - Andrew Jackson and his American army invade Florida in the Seminole War, causing repercussions with Spain as negotiations to purchase the territory had just begun.

April 4, 1818 - The flag of the United States is officially adopted by Congress with the configuration of thirteen red and white stripes and one star for each state in the union. At the time of adoption, with the most recent addition of Mississippi, the flag had twenty stars.

October 20, 1818 - The northern boundary of the United States and Canada is established between the U.S.A. and the United Kingdom. Its location from the Lake of the Woods to the Rocky Mountains would be the 49th parallel.

December 3, 1818 - The state of Illinois is admitted to the Union, making the U.S.A. a republic with twenty-one states.

The first edition of the Farmer's Almanac is published in Morristown, New Jersey.

1819
January 2, 1819 - The first financial crises in the United States, the Panic of 1819, occurs, leading to foreclosures, bank failures, and unemployment. Several causes have been identified, including the heavy amount of borrowing by the government to finance the War of 1812, as well as the tightening of credit by the Second Bank of the U.S. in response to risky lending practices by wildcat banks in the west.

February 15, 1819 - The Tallmadge Amendment is passed by the U.S. House of Representatives, stating that slaves would be barred in the new state of Missouri, which becomes the opening vote in the Missouri Compromise controversy.

February 22, 1819 - The territory of Florida is ceded to the United States by Spain.

May 22, 1819 - The American steamship Savannah, under part steam and sail-power, crosses the Atlantic Ocean from Savannah, Georgia to Liverpool, England, arriving on June 20.

August 6, 1819 - The first private military school in the United States, Norwich University, is founded by Captain Alden Partridge in Vermont.

1820

February 6, 1820 - Free African American colonists, eighty-six in number, plus three American Colonization society members, leave the United States from New York City and sail to Freetown, Sierra Leone.

March 3, 1820 - The Missouri Compromise bill, sponsored by Henry Clay, passes in the United States Congress. This legislation allows slavery in the Missouri territory, but not in any other location west of the Mississippi River that was north of 36 degrees 30 minutes latitude, the current southern line of the state of Missouri. The state of Missouri would be admitted to the Union, under this compromise, on August 10, 1821.

August 7, 1820 - Population in America continues to rise. The census of 1820 now includes 9,638,453 people living in the United States, 33% more than in 1810. The most populated state is New York, with 1,372,812 residents. The center of U.S. population now reaches 16 miles east of Moorefield, West Virginia.

September 28, 1820 - To prove that a tomato is not poisonous, Colonel Robert Gibbon Johnson eats one in public in Salem, Massachusetts.

November 1 to December 6, 1820 - The election of James Monroe to a second term in office comes with a landslide victory in the Electoral College with Monroe defeating John Quincy Adams by a tally of 231 to 1.

1821

February 23, 1821 - The first pharmacy college is founded in the Philadelphia College of Apothecaries. Also this same year, the first women's college in the United States of America, Troy Female Seminary, is founded by Emma Willard.

July 10, 1821 - Possession of the territory of Florida is taken by the United States after its purchase is completed with Spain. No money exchanged hands between Spain and the U.S. in this purchase; the U.S. had agreed to pay five million dollars to citizens for property damage.

August 4, 1821 - The Saturday Evening Post is published for the first time as a weekly newspaper by Atkinson and Alexander.

November 16, 1821 - The first legal international trade on the Santa Fe Trail began after William Becknell, a Missouri trader, met with Governor Melgares one day earlier. The huge profit earned convinced Becknell that he should return over the trail route the following year.

A Massachusetts court outlaws the novel, Fanny Hill, by John Cleland, and convicts publisher Peter Holmes for printing a "lewd and obscene" novel. This was the first obscenity case in U.S. history.

1822
January 7, 1822 - The first group of freed American slaves settle a black colony known as the Republic of Liberia when they arrive on African soil at Providence Island. The capital, Monrovia, is named after President James Monroe.

March 30, 1822 - Florida becomes an official territory of the United States.

April 27, 1822 - Civil War general and 18th President of the United States, Ulysses S. Grant, is born.

February 13, 1822 - Advertisements for Ashley's Hundred, organized by General William H. Ashley and Major Andrew Henry, to ascend the Missouri River on a fur trading mission, appear in Missouri newspapers. The men who would answer the call to employ included Jedediah Smith and Jim Bridger. Over the next decade, these expeditions would leave St. Louis at irregular intervals.

July 1822 - A law prohibiting the sale of alcohol to Indians is passed, causing a disruption in the fur trade pattern that relied on the Indians to trap and hunt for the furs, in exchange for alcohol and other goods.

1823

April 3, 1823 - American political boss, William Marcy Tweed, is born.

April 5, 1823 - Act signed for funding of the creation of the Albany Basin, a man-made port linked to the Erie Canal, in Albany, New York, is appropriated.

April 25, 1823 - The War Department issues order for an expedition up the Red River and along the 49th parallel led by Stephen Long, which would mark the point of the official border between the United States and Canada.

August 9, 1823 - Arikara Indian War begins as the U.S. Army engages in the first conflict with an Indian tribe in the western territories after the tribe had attacked a trapping party on June 1.

December 2, 1823 - In a speech before Congress, James Monroe announces the Monroe Doctrine, stating the policy that European intervention anyplace is the Americas is opposed and that he would establish American neutrality in future European wars.

1824

March 11, 1824 - The Bureau of Indian Affairs is established by the United States War Department. They appoint Ely Parker, a Seneca tribe member, as its first director. This department is meant to regulate trade with Indian tribes.

April 17, 1824 - A frontier treaty between the United States and Russia is signed, negotiated by Secretary of State under James Monroe, John Quincy Adams. Russia agreed to set its southern border at 54 degrees, 40 minutes and allow U.S. ships within the one hundred mile limit of its Pacific territories.

May 24, 1824 - In Pawtucket, Rhode Island, the first strike by female workers occurs.

December 2, 1824 - When the Electoral College vote yielded no majority, John Quincy Adams would be elected president by the House of Representatives on February 9, 1825, outpolling fellow Democrat Republicans, now a loose coalition of competing factions, including Andrew Jackson, who had actually received a higher number of Electoral College votes, 99, than Adams, 84. It was not a majority due to votes for Henry Clay, 37, and William Crawford, 41. In the first election with popular vote totals, Adams garnered less votes there as well, with 105,321 to 155,872 to Jackson.

December 24, 1824 - The first fraternity in the United States is begun, Chi Phi, at Princeton University.

1825
February 12, 1825 - In the state of Georgia, the Creek Indian tribe give up their last lands to the United States government and move west.

March 4, 1825 - John Quincy Adams is inaugurated as President, with John C. Calhoun as his Vice President after the House of Representatives settle the lack of an Electoral College majority.

October 26, 1825 - Use of the Erie Canal began in Buffalo, New York with the first boat departing for New York City. This opened up the Great Lakes region by cutting the travel time between the two cities one third and shipping costs nine tenths. Cost of the canal was $7 million. On November 4, 1825, the first boat navigating the Erie Canal arrived in New York City. The opening of the Erie Canal contributed to making the city of New York a chief Atlantic port.

November 26, 1825 - The first college social fraternity, Kappa Alpha, is formed at Union College, Schenectady, New York.

The first experimental steam locomotive is built and operated by John Stevens, of Hoboken, New Jersey.

1826
April 1, 1826 - The internal combustion engine named the "Gas Or Vapor Engine" is patented by American Samuel Morey.

July 4, 1826 - Two founding members of the United States pass away on Independence Day; Thomas Jefferson, 3rd President, and John Adams, 2nd President. On the same day, Stephen Foster, American songwriter and poet, is born.

September 3, 1826 - The first United States warship to navigate the world, the U.S.S. Vincennes, leaves New York City under the command of William Finch.

October 26, 1826 - Kit Carson, mountain man of the western lands, is wanted in Franklin, Missouri, after running away to join a trading party at the age of 16. A reward of one cent is offered for his return to his bondage to learn the saddler's job in Franklin.

In 1826, David Edward Jackson, for whom Jackson Hole, Wyoming is named, as well as Jedediah Smith and William Sublette purchase William Ashley's interest in the fur trade, and the company, later to become known as the Rocky Mountain Fur Company when these men sold in 1830, continued to profit from the fur trade across the mountain west.

1827
February 28, 1827 - The Baltimore and Ohio Railroad is incorporated, and would become the first railroad in the United States to offer transportation for people and commercial goods.

July 4, 1827 - In New York State, slavery is legally abolished.

July 14, 1827 - The first Roman Catholic Mass is held in the Hawaiian Islands and leads to the foundation of the Diocese of Honolulu.

September 22, 1827 - Joseph Smith, Jr. claims the angel Moroni gives him a record of gold plates, later translated into The Book of Mormon.

The Senate ratifies the Treaty of Limits that establishes the Sabine River as the Mexican and United States border, in agreement with the Adams-Onis Treaty of 1819.

1828
January 12, 1828 - The Treaty of Limits with Mexico goes into effect.

April 14, 1828 - The copyright for The American Dictionary of the English Language is registered and the book published that year by Noah Webster.

July 4, 1828 - The first passenger railroad in the United States, the Baltimore and Ohio, begins.

October 31 to December 2, 1828 - After a tumultuous four years of national politics, the election for president sees a popular and electoral college vote victory of 178-83 for Andrew Jackson over President John Quincy Adams.

October 28, 1828 - Opposing the Tariff of Abominations, the state of South Carolina begins the process of a formal nullification campaign, declaring the right of state nullification of federal laws.

1829

February 26, 1829 - Levi Strauss, American clothing designer and jeans entrepreneur, is born. He would be credited with manufacturing the first blue jeans.

March 4, 1829 - Andrew Jackson, now in the Democratic party, is inaugurated as President, replacing John Quincy Adams after his sole term in office.

June 1, 1829 - The Philadelphia Inquirer newspaper is founded. It was initially known as the Pennsylvania Inquirer.

June 27, 1829 - The Smithsonian Institution is founded when British scientist James Smithson bequeathed one hundred thousand pounds ($500,000) from his estate for its initial funding, on the condition that his nephew have no heirs. The establishment of the Smithsonian would be passed by an act of Congress in 1846 and was completed in 1855. The Smithsonian complex, on the National Mall in Washington, D.C., now includes 19 museums and 142 million items in their collection.

July 23, 1829 - William Austin Burt, of the United States, invents and patents the typewriter, at the time called the typographer.

1830
April 6, 1830 - Joseph Smith organizes the Mormon Church, known as the Church of Jesus Christ of Latter-Day Saints, in Fayette, New York. He had published the Book of Mormon on March 26, 1830.

May 26, 1830 - The United States Congress approved the Indian Removal Act, which facilitated the relocation of Indian tribes from east of the Mississippi River. Although this act did not order their removal, it paved the way for increased pressure on Indian tribes to accept land-exchange treaties with the U.S. government and helped lead the way to the Trail of Tears.

June 1, 1830 - The United States continues to expand, increasing its population 33% in one decade to 12,860,702 in the 1830 census. The center of U.S. population moved west, but only slightly, to a point nineteen miles west, southwest of Moorefield, West Virginia.

William L. Sublette, with the goods from the Rocky Mountain Fur Company (known as from 1830-1833), took the first wagons along the Oregon Trail to the Rocky Mountains, diverting at South Pass as he went to the 1830 trade rendezvous at the Little Wind River in present-day Wyoming. The supply caravan included eighty-one men on mules, ten wagons, and two carriages.

December 10, 1830 - American poet, Emily Dickinson, is born.

1831
March 19, 1831 - The first bank robbery in United States history occurs at the City Bank of New York. Edward Smith robbed the Wall Street bank of $245,000. He would be caught and convicted of the crime with sentencing of five years in Sing Sing prison.

May 27, 1831 - Jedediah Smith, legendary mountain man and fur trader with the Rocky Mountain Fur Company, is killed by Comanche on the Cimarron River. The expeditions by Smith were noted as the most dangerous explorations during the height of the fur trade years.

June 30, 1831 - At Arlington, Virginia, overlooking the capitol at Washington, D.C., Robert E. Lee, then a lieutenant in the Federal Army, married a great-granddaughter of Martha Washington, Mary Custis.

August 21, 1831 - A local slave rebellion in Southampton County, Virginia, led by Nat Turner, a black slave, kills fifty-seven white citizens. Turner would be captured on October 30 of the same year, tried, and hanged on November 11 for his part in the uprising.

Cyrus H. McCormick, U.S inventor, invented and demonstrated the first commercially successful reaper, picking up where his father left off. He developed the reaper over six weeks time with the assistance of his black helper Jo Anderson. The reaper would be used in their 1831 harvest in the Shenandoah Valley of Virginia. McCormick would patent the reaper in 1834.

1832
April 20, 1832 - The first act of Congress to protect a natural resource was signed by President Andrew Jackson. It reserved four parcels of land with hot mineral springs in Arkansas Territory at Hot Springs.

April 8, 1832 - The Black Hawk War begins and would rage from Illinois to Wisconsin through September. It would consequently lead to the removal of Sauk and Fox Indians west, across the Mississippi River.

July 24, 1832 - The first wagons crossed the Continental Divide on the Oregon Trail at Wyoming's South Pass when Captain Benjamin Bonneville and Joseph R. Walker navigated one hundred and ten men with twenty-one wagons into the Green River Valley.

October 8-10, 1832 - The six year campaign known as the Trail of Tears begins when Washington Irving, Henry Levitt Ellsworth, and Captain Jesse Bean, at the Arkansas River, begin one of the first steps in the U.S. campaign to remove Indians from their homes on the east coast.

November 1832 - South Carolina convention passed the Ordinance of Nullification, which was against the institution of permanent tariffs. The state also, on this issue, threatened to withdraw from the union of the United States of America.

1833
March 1, 1833 - The United States Congress passed a compromise tariff act in response to South Carolina's objections. The state of South Carolina subsequently withdrew the Nullification Ordinance upon its approval.

March 2, 1833 - The Force Bill is signed by President Andrew Jackson, which would authorize him to use troops to enforce Federal law in South Carolina, if necessary.

March 4, 1833 - The second term inauguration occurs for President Jackson, with Martin Van Buren as Vice President after the resignation on December 28, 1832 of John Calhoun as Vice President. Jackson had won a convincing victory in the November election. His defeat of Henry Clay and the National Republicans saw an Electoral College vote of 219 to 49. He also won the popular vote victory.

June 24, 1833 - The United States frigate Constitution, "Old Ironsides," was retired to the initial naval drydock at the Charlestown Naval Yard in New England, where it remains on exhibit as part of Boston's history.

September 2, 1833 - Oberlin College is founded. It refused to bar students on the subject of race and included the distinction of becoming the first college in the United States to offer coeducation.

1834
January 3, 1834 - Stephen F. Austin, the Father of Texas, is imprisoned by Mexican government officials in Mexico City for insurrection. He was not tried and finally returned to Texas in August 1835.

March 18, 1834 - Pennsylvania's Main Line canal was linked between Philadelphia and Pittsburgh by a system of ten inclined planes which crossed the Allegheny Mountains and began operations.

March 28, 1834 - The United States Senate censured President Andrew Jackson for de-funding the Second Bank of the United States.

John Jacob Astor, a German immigrant, was commonly known as the richest man in the United States. He was the organizer of the American Fur Company, which he sold in 1834.

October 14, 1834 - Henry Blair receives the second patent awarded to an African American when he patents a corn planter.

1835
January 30, 1835 - In the United States Capitol, Andrew Jackson encounters an unsuccessful assassination attempt from an unemployed house painter, Richard Lawrence. Jackson, after two point-blank shots misfired, confronted his attacker with a cane. This was the first attempt on the life of a President of the United States.

June 2, 1835 - P.T. Barnum begins his first circus tour of the United States.

October 2, 1835 - The Revolution of Texas begins with the Battle of Gonzales when Mexican soldiers try to disarm the people of Gonzales, but are resisted by local militia. By November, Texas proclaimed the right to secede from Mexico with Sam Houston taking command of the Texas army. His Texas army would capture San Antonio on December 9.

December 16, 1835 - A fire in New York City rages, eventually destroying 530 buildings, including the New York Stock Exchange.

December 29, 1835 - The Cherokee tribe is forced to cede lands in Georgia and cross the Mississippi River after gold is found on their land in Georgia, which results in the Treaty of New Echota.

1836
February 3, 1836 - The first convention of the American Whig

Party is held in Albany, New York.

February 23 - March 6, 1836 - The battle for the Alamo is waged in San Antonio, Texas when 3,000 Mexican troops under Santa Ana attack the mission and its 189 defenders. Texas troops lose the battle after a thirteen day siege. On March 2, 1836, Texas independence was declared at a convention of delegates from fifty-seven Texas communities at Washington-on-the-Brazos, making them an independent nation free from Mexican rule.

February 25, 1836 - The patent for the first revolver is awarded to inventor Samuel Colt.

April 21, 1836 - The battle of San Jacinto is waged with Sam Houston leading the Texas army to victory over Mexican forces. Santa Ana and his troops are taken prisoner the next day along the San Jacinto River.

July 11, 1836 - The Specie Act is issued by executive order of President Andrew Jackson. This act would lead to the failure of the economy of land speculation and the Panic of 1837.

December 7, 1836 - Martin Van Buren continues the victories for the Democratic party in the November presidential election, defeating William H. Harrison, a Whig, 170 to 73 in the Electoral College vote.

1837
February 25, 1837 - The patent for the first United States electronic printing press is awarded to Thomas Davenport.

March 4, 1837 - Martin Van Buren, as President, and Richard M. Johnson, Vice President, are inaugurated into office.

March 4, 1837 - The city of Chicago is granted a charter by Illinois.

May 10, 1837 - The global economic crises known as the Panic of 1837 begins with the failure of New York City banks and unemployment which would reach record levels.

November 7, 1837 - Elijah P. Lovejoy, an abolitionist printer, is killed by a mob of slavery supporters, when he was trying to protect his shop from its third destruction.

1838
January 4, 1838 - Tom Thumb, the American circus performer, is born.

January 6, 1838 - Samuel Morse, a portrait painter who later turned to invention, first publicly demonstrated the telegraph and developed the Morse Code system of communication. He would apply for a patent two years later in 1840.

June 12, 1838 - The Territory of Iowa is organized.

September 3, 1838 - Frederick Douglass, future abolitionist, boards a train in Maryland to freedom from slavery, with borrowed identification and a sailor's uniform from a free Black seaman.

October 27, 1838 - Missouri governor Lilburn Boggs issues an order for the expulsion of Mormons from the state of Missouri.

1839
February 11, 1839 - The first university west of the Mississippi River is established, the University of Missouri.

February 15, 1839 - In Jackson, Mississippi, the first state law allowing women to own property is passed.

February 24, 1839 - Americans invent. William Otis receives a patent for the steam shovel. Later that year, American inventor Thaddeus Fairbanks invented the platform scales and Charles Goodyear invented rubber vulcanization.

November 11, 1839 - In Lexington, Virginia, the Virginia Military Institute is founded.

During the decade of the 1830's, German American immigrants introduced the tradition of decorating Christmas trees during the holidays to America.

1840
January 13, 1840 - Off the coast of Long Island, New York, 139 people lose their lives when the steamship Lexington burns and sinks four miles off the coast.

January 19, 1840 - Antarctica is claimed for the United States when Captain Charles Wilkes circumnavigates the continent and claims Wilkes Land for the nation.

June 1, 1840 - The census of the United States grows to 17,063,353, up 33% from the decade before. Four states now exceed one million in population; New York, Pennsylvania, Ohio and Virginia. The center of the nation's population continues to move slowly west, now sixteen miles south of Clarksburg, West Virginia.

May 7, 1840 - The Great Natchez Trace Tornado strikes Natchez, Mississippi and wreaks havoc. In the second most deadly tornado in U.S. history, 317 people are counted among the dead and 209 are injured.

December 2, 1840 - President Martin Van Buren is defeated for reelection by William Henry Harrison. Harrison, a Whig, receives 234 Electoral College votes to 60 and also wins the popular vote contest.

1841
February 18, 1841 - The first ongoing filibuster begins in the United States Senate and lasts until March 11.

March 9, 1841 - The Supreme Court of the U.S. states that in the case of the slave ship Amistad that the Africans who had wrested control of the ship had been bound into slavery illegally.

April 4, 1841 - President William Henry Harrison, sworn into office only one month before on March 4, dies of pneumonia. His tenure of one month is the shortest in history and his death in office the first for a president of the United States. He is succeeded by Vice President John Tyler.

May 1, 1841 - The first wagon train, with sixty-nine adults and several children, leave for California from Independence, Missouri. The journey would take until November 4.

August 16, 1841 - President Tyler vetoes the bill re-establishing the Second Bank of the United States, causing an angry riot among Whig party members on White House grounds. It was the most violent demonstration on those grounds in U.S. history.

1842
January 31, 1842 - Elizabeth Tyler, the president's daughter, marries William Nevison Walker, at the White House in Washington, D.C.

March 5, 1842 - In a prelude four years prior to the start of the Mexican War, troops under Mexican leader Rafael Vasquez invade Texas and briefly occupy San Antonio in the first invasion since the Texas Revolution.

May 16, 1842 - The second organized wagon train on the Oregon Trail leaves with more than one hundred pioneers from Elm Grove, Missouri. Although not welcomed due to company policy that discouraged emigration, they were offered food and farming equipment at Fort Vancouver by the Hudson Bay Company upon arrival.

May 19, 1842 - The People's Party of Providence, Rhode Island, founded by lawyer Thomas Wilson Dorr in 1841, wanted to liberalize the Rhode Island charter of 1663 to extend voting to those that didn't own property. The Dorr Rebellion of 1842 of this date, with militiamen attacking an arsenal in Providence that was later repulsed, however, forced conservatives to abolish the charter and adopt a new constitution one year later.

August 9, 1842 - The border between the United States and Canada is fixed east of the Rocky Mountains, including Maine and Minnesota, due to the signing of the Webster-Ashburton Treaty.

November 26, 1842 - The University of Notre Dame is founded by Father Edward Sorin of the Congregation of the Holy Cross. The University would be granted a charter by the state of Indiana two years later.

1843
February 6, 1843 - At the Bowery Amphitheatre in New York City, the first minstrel show in the United States debuts.

May 22, 1843 - The first major wagon train headed for the northwest via the Oregon Trail begins with one thousand pioneers from Elm Grove, Missouri.

June 4, 1843 - The Black Horse Troop of the 1st United States Dragoons from Fort Scott, Kansas join a military escort into Indian Territory along the Santa Fe Trail and apprehend Jacob Snively and his Texas freebooters.

June 21, 1843 - Edgar Allan Poe publishes his story The Gold Bug in the Dollar Newspaper. He is paid more than a dollar, however, winning the grand prize of $100.

November 28, 1843 - The Kingdom of Hawaii is officially recognized by European nations as an independent nation. This date signifies Hawaiian Independence Day.

1844
April 6, 1844 - Edgar Allan Poe, the highly regarded writer of short stories, departs his home in Philadelphia for New York City. Although most of this best works were written while in the City of Brotherly Love for two years, he left the city with $4.50 to his name.

May 24, 1844 - Samuel B. Morse, inventor of the telegraph, sends the first message over the first telegraph line from Washington to Baltimore. His words were, "What God hath wrought."

June 15, 1844 - The patent for vulcanization, the process for strengthening rubber, is granted to Charles Goodyear.

July 3, 1844 - The United States signs the treaty of Wanghia with China. It is the first treaty signed between the two nations.

December 4, 1844 - Democrat James K. Polk defeats Henry Clay for president with 170 Electoral College votes to 105 for Clay.

1845
March 3, 1845 - Congress overrides a presidential veto. President Tyler's veto of a military appropriation was overturned.

July 4, 1845 - The Congress of Texas votes for annexation to the United States of America with the majority of voters in Texas approving a constitution on October 13. These actions followed the signing of a bill by President Tyler on March 1, authorizing the United States to annex the Republic of Texas and led to the United States adding the Republic of Texas into the Union as the 28th state on December 29.

October 21, 1845 - The New York Herald becomes the first newspaper to mention the game of baseball. In this year, Alexander Cartwright and his New York Knickerbockers baseball team codify the "rules of baseball" for the first time, including nine men per side.

December 2, 1845 - U.S. President Polk invokes the concept of Manifest Destiny, announcing to Congress that the Monroe Doctrine should be strictly enforced and that the settlement of the West should be aggressively pursued.

American inventor Elias Howe, working as a machinist after losing his factory job in the Panic of 1837, invents his sewing machine. Howe would patent the device on September 10, 1846.

1846
January 5, 1846 - The United States House of Representatives changes its policy toward sharing the Oregon Territory with the United Kingdom. On June 15, the Oregon Treaty is signed with Great Britain, fixing the boundary of the United States and Canada at the 49th parallel from the Rocky Mountains to the Straits of Juan de Fuca.

May 8, 1846 - The first conflict of the Mexican War occurs north of the Rio Grande River at Palo Alto, Texas when United States troops under the command of Major General Zachary Taylor rout a larger Mexican force. Zachary had been ordered by President Polk to seize disputed Texas land settled by Mexicans. War is declared by the United States against Mexico on May 13, backed by southerners while northern Whigs were in opposition. Ten days later, Mexico declares war back.

June 10, 1846 - The Republic of California declares independence from Mexico. Four days later, the bear flag of the Republic of California is raised at Sonoma.

July 28, 1846 - The Army of the West, under the command of Brigadier General Stephen Watts Kearny, travel down the Santa Fe Trail and arrive at Bent's Old Fort en route to the conquest of New Mexico.

August 14, 1846 - South of the town of Cape Girardeau in Missouri, the Cape Girardeau meteorite strikes. It is a 2.3 kg chondrite type meteorite.

1847
March 27-29, 1847 - Twelve thousand American troops under the command of General Winfield Scott take Vera Cruz, Mexico after a siege.

May 7, 1847 - The American Medical Association is founded in Philadelphia.

July 1, 1847 - The first adhesive postage stamps in the United States went on sale with Benjamin Franklin gracing the 5 cent stamp and George Washington fronting the 10 cent stamp.

July 24, 1847 - One hundred and forty-eight Mormons under Brigham Young settle at Salt Lake City, Utah after leaving Nauvoo, Illinois for the west on February 10, 1846 due to violent clashes over their beliefs, which included the practice of polygamy through the end of the 1800s.

September 8-15, 1847 - The Battle for Mexico City is fought, beginning two miles outside the city at King's Mill. The main assault against the fortress Capultepec came on September 12 under the command of General Winfield Scott, with combatants including Ulysses S. Grant and John Quitman's 4th Division, of which George Pickett and James Longstreet were a part. Quitman's division entered a deserted city, which had been

abandoned by Santa Anna's forces during the night on
September 15.

1848
January 12, 1848 - Abraham Lincoln, as Congressman from
Springfield, Illinois, attacked President Polk's handling of the
Mexican War in a speech in the House of Representatives.

January 24, 1848 - Gold was discovered in California by James
W. Marshall at Sutter's Mill in the town of Colona. Seven months
later, on August 19, the New York Herald breaks the news of the
gold rush to East Coast readers, prompting eighty thousand
prospectors to flood California and the Barbary Coast of San
Francisco in 1849.

February 2, 1848 - The Treaty of Guadalupe Hidalgo ended the
Mexican War with Mexico relinquishing its rights to Texas above
the Rio Grande River and ceding New Mexico and California to
the United States. The United States also gained claims to
Arizona, Nevada, Utah, and part of Colorado. In exchange, the
United States assumed $3 million in American claims and paid
Mexico $15 million. The treaty is ratified one month later on
March 10 by the U.S. Senate. Mexico would ratify the treaty on
May 19.

July 20, 1848 - The Declaration of Sentiments calling for equal
rights for women and men is signed by 100 men and women in
the Wesleyan Methodist Chapel, Seneca Falls, New York at the
1st Women's Rights Convention led by Lucretia Mott and
Elizabeth Cady Stanton.

November 7, 1848 - Zachary Taylor, hero of the Mexican War,
defeats Lewis Cass in the presidential election of 1848. Whig
Taylor garners 163 Electoral College votes to 127 for the
Democratic candidate. This was the first U.S. election held on the
same date in every state.

1849
January 23, 1849 - The first woman doctor in the United States,
Elizabeth Blackwell, is granted her degree by the Medical
Institute of Geneva, New York.

April 4, 1849 - The first baseball uniforms are introduced by the New York Knickerbockers club; blue and white cricket outfits were used.

February 28, 1849 - With the arrival of the SS California in San Francisco after a four month twenty-one day journey around the Cape Horn from New York City, regular steamboat service is inaugurated between the east and west coasts.

March 3, 1849 - The United States Department of the Interior is established.

December 4, 1849 - Crazy Horse, Chief of the Oglala Sioux, is born.

1850
January 29, 1850 - Debate on the future of slavery in the territories escalates when Henry Clay introduces the Compromise of 1850 to the U.S. Congress. On March 7, Senator Daniel Webster endorses the bill as a measure to avert a possible civil war.

June 1, 1850 - The United States census of 1850 counts 23,191,876 population, a 35.9% increase from a decade before. Over three million people now live in its most populous state, New York.

July 10, 1850 - Millard Fillmore is sworn into office as the 13th President of the United States after the death of Zachary Taylor the day before. His policies on the topic of slavery did not appease expansionists or slave-holders.

September 9, 1850 - The Compromise of 1850, pushed by Senator Henry Clay, admits California as the 31st state, without slavery, and adds Utah and New Mexico as territories with no decision on the topic. The Fugitive Slave Law is strengthened under the Compromise, which also ended the slave trade in the District of Columbia.

September 11, 1850 - P.T. Barnum, entrepreneur extra ordinaire, introduces the Swedish Nightingale, Jenny Lind, to an American audience of six thousand at a charge of $3 per person (and more). Her debut at Castle Garden, a converted fort on Manhattan Island, is a rousing success.

1851
May 1, 1851 - The United States of America participates in the opening ceremony of the first World's Fair in history, the Great Exhibition of the Works of Industry of All Nations, in the Crystal Palace designed by Joseph Paxton, in Hyde Park, London, England. The world's fair becomes the first major gathering of the works of nations in one location under the idea of Prince Albert and support of Queen Victoria.

August 22, 1851 - The America's Cup yachting race is

inaugurated with the victor crowned in the yacht aptly named, "America."

October 11, 1851 - The first world's fair closes after 141 days of exhibition. 6,039,195 visitors attend the Crystal Palace exhibition, held on twenty-six acres in London's Hyde Park, with exhibits from fifty nations and thirty-nine colonies. The United States had 499 exhibits, of which McCormick's reaper won a gold medal and Charles Goodyear a council medal. To this day, profits from the first world exposition still provide funds for scholarships and cultural endowments throughout England, and this exhibition would spawn over one hundred more, including expos in Shanghai, China in 2010, Yeosu, South Korea in 2012, and Milan, Italy in 2015.

November 14, 1851 - The American publishing industry manufactures Herman Melville's "Moby Dick." The industry also publishes Nathanial Hawthorne's "House of Seven Gables," in 1851, and the painting of "Washington Crossing the Delaware" is completed by German-American artist Emmanuel Leutze.

December 29, 1851 - The first YMCA opens in Boston, Massachusetts.

1852
February 16, 1852 - The Studebaker Brothers Wagon Company is established and would become the largest producer in the world of wagons.

February 19, 1852 - At Jefferson College in Canonsburg, Pennsylvania, the Phi Kappa Psi fraternity is begun.

March 20, 1852 - Harriet Beecher Stowe's masterpiece of American slavery, Uncle Tom's Cabin, is published. Stowe wrote this work of anti-slavery in response to the Fugitive Slave Act. It sold 300,000 copies in its first years of publication.

June 29, 1852 - American Senator Henry Clay, author of much legislation on the topic of slavery, dies. Later that year, on October 24, statesman Daniel Webster, would also pass away. This void in American politics would be felt throughout the next decade as the difficult days of slavery and Civil War would consume the nation.

November 2, 1852 - Franklin Pierce, a Democrat, wins a convincing victory for President, defeating Whig Winfield Scott by a tally of 254 to 42 electoral votes. He also garners the majority in the popular vote. His four years as President, which began March 4, 1853, would cause dismay among Democrats, who would fail to nominate him for office again in 1856.

1853

January 11, 1853 - John Ericsson, designer of the ironclad Monitor one decade later, tests his ship powered by a caloric, hot air, engine in New York Harbor, but the experiment fails due to lack of power.

April 22, 1853 - The Indian Frontier Post, Fort Scott, in Indian Territory (Kansas) is evacuated by the United States Army riflemen.

July 8, 1853 - Commodore Matthew C. Perry and the United States Navy arrive in Edo Bay, Japan. They would negotiate a treaty to allow U.S. ships into Japan.

July 14, 1853 - U.S. President Franklin Pierce opens the first world's fair held in the United States, the Exhibition of the Industry of All Nations. Located on 6th Avenue in a large palace on the site of the current New York Public Library, twenty-three foreign nations and colonies participated.

December 30, 1853 - The Gadsden Purchase is consummated, with the United States buying a 29,640 square mile tract of land in present-day Arizona and New Mexico (approximately from Yuma to Las Cruces) for $10 million from Mexico to allow railroad building in the southwest and settle continued border disputes after the Mexican-American War. This act finalized the borders of the Continental United States.

1854

February 28, 1854 - In Ripon, Wisconsin, the Republican Party is founded, in opposition to the Kansas-Nebraska Act. It would hold its first convention later that year on July 6 in Jackson, Michigan.

May 30, 1854 - The Kansas-Nebraska act becomes law, allowing the issue of slavery to be decided by a vote of settlers. This established the territories of Kansas and Nebraska and would breed much of the rancor that culminated in the actions of the next years of "Bleeding Kansas."

June 10, 1854 - The United States Naval Academy graduates its first class at Annapolis, Maryland.

October 26, 1854 – C. W. Post, American cereal manufacturer, is born.

October 31, 1854 - The New York World's Fair, extended for a second season, closes after 393 exhibit days. The second season, under the presidency of P.T. Barnum, raises the total attendance to over 1,150,000.

1855
March 3, 1855 - The United States Camel Corps is created with a $30,000 appropriation in Congress.

March 24, 1855 - American businessman, banker and philanthropist, Andrew Mellon, is born.

April 21, 1855 - The first railroad train crosses the Mississippi River on the first bridge constructed at Rock Island, Illinois to Davenport, Iowa.

July 1, 1855 - Quinault River Treaty between the United States and the Quinault and Quileute tribes of the Olympic Peninsula in Washington Territory cedes their lands to the United States. It was a goal of territorial governors at the time to acquire land cession treaties with Native Americans.

October 9, 1855 - The Shuttle Sewing Machine and its machine motor are patented by Isaac M. Singer, improving the development of the sewing machine.

1856
April 5, 1856 - Booker T. Washington was born in slavery on a tobacco farm in Franklin County, Virginia, and would later emerge as one of the foremost black leaders and educators of

the 20th century.

May 21, 1856 - Pro-slavery forces under Sheriff Samuel J. Jones burn the Free-State Hotel and destroy two anti-slavery newspapers and other businesses in Lawrence, Kansas. Three days later, the Pottowatomie Massacre occurs in Franklin County, Kansas when followers of abolitionist John Brown kill five homesteaders.

May 22, 1856 - South Carolina Congressman Preston Brooks attacks Senator Charles Sumner with a cane in the hall of the U.S. Senate after Sumner gave a speech attacking Southern sympathizers for the pro-slavery violence in Kansas. Sumner would take three years to recover while Brooks was lionized throughout Southern states.

November 4, 1856 - John C. Fremont, the first candidate for president under the banner of the Republican Party, loses his bid for the presidency to James C. Buchanan, despite support for Fremont from Abraham Lincoln. Buchanan, the only bachelor to become president as well as the sole Pennsylvanian garnered 174 Electoral College votes to 114 for Fremont. Millard Fillmore, running on the American Know-Nothing and Whig tickets was also defeated.

November 17, 1856 - Fort Buchanan is established by the U.S. Army on the Sonoita River in current southern Arizona to administrate the new land bought in the Gadsden Purchase.

1857
March 4, 1857 - James Buchanan is sworn into office as the 15th President of the United States. His tenure as President would be marred by the question of slavery and a compromise stance that would neither alleviate nor eradicate the intractable question from American society.

March 6, 1857 - The United States Supreme Court rules in the Dred Scott decision, 6-3, that a slave did not become free when transported into a free state. It also ruled that slavery could not be banned by the U.S. Congress in a territory, and that blacks were not eligible to be awarded citizenship.

March 23, 1857 - The first elevator is installed by Elisha Otis on Broadway in New York City.

August 11, 1857 - Colonel Isaac Neff Ebey, leader of the first permanent white settlers to Whidbey Island, Washington Territory seven years earlier, is beheaded and shot by Indian raiders.

December 21, 1857 - Two companies of the 1st Cavalry under Captain Samuel Sturgis arrive at Fort Scott, Kansas to attempt to bring the disorder of "Bleeding Kansas," the slavery versus anti-slavery battle, in check.

1858
April 28, 1858 - Frederick Law Olmsted and Calvert Vaux, landscape architects, win the competition and adoption of their plan for Central Park in New York City.

June 23, 1858 - With strife between pro-slavery and anti-slavery partisans escalating to dramatic chaos, the 2nd Infantry and 3rd Artillery regiments under the command of Captain Nathanial Lyon attempt to restore order during the "Bleeding Kansas" campaign.

August 5, 1858 - The first transatlantic cable is completed by Cyrus West Field and others. It would fail its test due to weak current on September 1.

August 21 to October 15, 1858 - A series of seven debates between politicians Stephen Douglas and Abraham Lincoln occur in Illinois.

September 17, 1858 - Dred Scott, the American slave who precipitated the decision by the Supreme Court on the topic of slavery, dies.

1859
February 14, 1859 - Oregon is admitted to the Union as the 33rd state.

August 27, 1859 - The first productive oil well for commercial use is drilled by Edwin L. Drake in Titusville, Pennsylvania.

October 16, 1859 - The United States Armory at the confluence of the Shenandoah and Potomac Rivers at Harper's Ferry, Virginia (now West Virginia) is seized by twenty-one men under the leadership of abolitionist John Brown. This act to cause an uprising of slaves in the surrounding territories fails when federal troops on October 18, under the command of Colonel Robert E. Lee, kill several of the raiders and capture John Brown. The town of Harper's Ferry, now a spectacular National Park on the topic, remains one of the under recognized historic treasures in the United States.

November 1, 1859 - The Cape Lookout, North Carolina lighthouse, with a Fresnel lens seen nineteen miles away, is lit for the first time.

December 2, 1859 - John Brown is hanged for treason by the state of Virginia due to his leadership role in the raid on the Harper's Ferry armory and failed attempt to spur revolt among Virginia slaves.

<u>U.S. Timeline: The 1860s - The Civil War</u>

1860
February 22, 1860 - Twenty thousand New England shoe workers strike and subsequently win higher wages.

April 3, 1860 - The Pony Express begins. Overland mail between Sacramento, California and St. Joseph's, Missouri is carried over the Oregon Trail for eighteen months by this series of riders on horseback, then rendered obsolete when the transcontinental telegraph is completed. Service ended on October 24, 1861.

Emmanuel Leutze is commissioned by Congress and begins to paint the mural, "Westward Ho the Course of Empire Takes Its Way," in July 1861 for the U.S. Capitol. The mural represents frontier settlement.

November 6, 1860 - Republican candidate Abraham Lincoln, running on an anti-slavery platform, defeats three opponents in the campaign for the presidency; Democrats Stephen A. Douglas and John C. Breckinridge, and John Bell, Constitutional Union Party, leading to ardent cries of potential rebellion in southern slave states. Although Lincoln won the Electoral College by a large majority, 180 to 123 for all other candidates, the popular vote showed just how split the nation was. Lincoln garnered 1.9 million votes to the 2.8 million spread amongst his opponents.

December 20, 1860 - South Carolina responds to the election of Abraham Lincoln as President by being the first southern state to secede from the Union.

1861
February 4, 1861 - In Montgomery, Alabama, the convention to form the Confederated States of America opens. Four days later, with Jefferson Davis as president, seven southern states officially set up the C.S.A.

March 4, 1861 - Abraham Lincoln is sworn in as president of the United States with Hannibal Hamlin as Vice President.

April 12, 1861 - Fort Sumter in Charleston, South Carolina harbor is bombarded for 34 hours by Confederate forces after the U.S.

Army commander failed to evacuate, thus starting the four years of conflict and the U.S. Civil War. The Confederate States of America, formed two months earlier had sought to force federal troops from occupation of its territory. Fort Sumter was captured April 14 when Major Robert Anderson turned the fort over to the Confederacy.

April 15, 1861 - President Lincoln calls for 75,000 volunteers to fight the secessionist activities in the Confederated States of America, which rose to eleven southern states in secession by May.

July 21, 1861 - The first Battle of Bull Run at Manassas, Virginia occurs with the repulsion of Union forces by the Confederacy. Led by generals such as Stonewall Jackson, the overwhelming defeat by the Confederate forces of the Union, seen by onlookers who viewed the battle as nothing more than an exercise that would be easily won, showed vibrant indication that the Civil War would not be over quickly or without much cost.

1862
March 9, 1862 - The USS Monitor won the battle against the Confederate ironclad Virginia off the coast of Hampton Roads, Virginia.

April 7, 1862 - The Army of the Tennessee, under General Grant, repulses the Confederate advance of the day earlier at the Battle of Shiloh, Tennessee, one of the largest battles of the western theatre in the U.S. Civil War. This battle, along with the unconditional surrender of Fort Donelson to General Grant on February 16, signaled the first major successes of the Union army in the west.

May 20, 1862 - The Homestead Act is approved, granting family farms of 160 acres (65 hectares) to settlers, many of which were carved from Indian territories. Two months later, on July 7, the Land Grant Act was approved, which called for public land sale to fund agricultural education. This act eventually led to the establishment of the state university systems.

September 17, 1862 - Emboldened by the victory at 2nd Manassas at the end of August, Confederate troops began the

1st invasion of Northern territory. Begun with a skirmish the night before north of Sharpsburg, Maryland, the day of September 17 along Antietam Creek burns bright as the bloodiest day of the Civil War. Along the Bloody Lane of the Sunken Road, around the Dunker Church, on the bluffs above Burnside Bridge, and in the ripped stalks of the cornfield, Union and Confederate troops fell in astounding numbers. Considered a victory by Union forces when the Confederates abandoned the field, even though Southern troops marching from Harper's Ferry had stemmed the Union tide the night before, Antietam is known for several other outcomes, including McClellan's lack of pursuit of the enemy which would eventually lead to his dismissal, as well as a victory that stemmed the tide of Confederate advance to the north, and allowed the announcement of the Emancipation Proclamation.

September 22, 1862 - President Abraham Lincoln, fresh on the heals of the Antietam victory, issues the preliminary Emancipation Proclamation, stating that all slaves in places of rebellion against the Federal Government would be free as of January 1, 1863.

December 11, 1862 - General Ambrose Burnside begins the Battle of Fredericksburg when Union troops cross the Rappahannock River on pontoons, leading two days later to an ignominious and one-sided defeat by General Robert E. Lee. At locations such as Marye's Heights, Union troops engaged in futile and deathly charges against fortified positions only to be repulsed again and again. Subsequent withdraw to the other side of the river signaled Burnside's defeat, and the mud march of later days only underscores the mire of his decisions during the battle.

1863
January 1, 1863 - Daniel Freeman files one of the first homestead applications at the Brownsville Land Office in Nebraska, cementing the Homestead Act of 1862 on its first day of implementation. The Emancipation Proclamation goes into effect.

July 1-3, 1863 - After three days of battle surrounding the tiny town of Gettysburg, including over 150,000 troops, Union defenders of Cemetery Ridge turn back General Pickett and Pettigrew during Pickett's Charge. With over 51,000 dead, wounded, or missing, the Battle of Gettysburg, on the farm fields of central Pennsylvania, proved to be the "high water mark of the Confederacy" and the last major push of Confederate forces into Union territory. Gettysburg remains a tribute of remarkable proportion to the men who fought and died on its fields, containing a reverence to the battle that played a major part in retaining the character of the United States of America.

July 4, 1863 - The city of Vicksburg surrenders to General Grant after a two month siege. The Vicksburg campaign included major battles from May 19, including the sinking of gunboats on the Mississippi River by Confederate defenders. This major accomplishment in the western theatre, plus the actions of Meade at Gettysburg one day earlier with the repulse of Pickett's Charge, prove to be the two most important victories of the Civil War. Even though it would take nearly two more years for the Confederate States of America to be defeated, these nearly simultaneous Union victories turned out to be the apex of the separatists.

July 13-16, 1863 - The New York draft riots kill about 1,000 people. Rioters protested the draft provision that allowed for money to be paid to get out of service. These payments would cease in 1864.

November 19, 1863 - "Four score and seven years ago," began what many perceive as the best speech in American history, delivered by President Abraham Lincoln in the town cemetery overlooking the fields of Gettysburg. The Gettysburg Address, only 272 words long and taking about two minutes to speak, captured the essence of the Civil War as both sacrifice and inspiration.

November 24, 1863 - Union General George Thomas scaled the heights of Chattanooga during one of the most arduous military charges in history. This charge caused Confederate forces to abandon the area, leaving Chattanooga and the majority of Tennessee under Union control.

1864
May 5-12, 1864 - At the Battles of the Wilderness and Spotsylvania, General Grant, now the first three star lieutenant

general since George Washington and in charge of the U.S. Army, marched against the forces of General Lee in a remarkable series of clashes within the dense forests of Virginia. Union casualties alone numbered nearly 3,000 dead, 21,000 wounded, and 4,000 missing.

July 14, 1864 - In an attempt to cut the railroad supply route and stop General William T. Sherman's march on Atlanta, Lt. General Nathan Bedford Forrest engaged Union forces in the Battle of Tupelo, Mississippi. By the end of September 1st, Sherman had taken Atlanta and by December 22, Savannah was subdued.

September 29, 1864 - Union forces, including black Union soldiers, capture the Confederate Fort Harrison, south of Richmond. This caused a Confederate realignment of their southern defenses.

November 8, 1864 - President Lincoln defeats former Union General George B. McClellan to remain president of the United States, a repudiation of the tactics of delay favored by his former commander, and a signal of support for the President as he continued to prosecute the rebellion by the southern Confederate states. Lincoln receives 2.2 million votes and 212 in the electoral college compared to 1.8 million votes and 21 in the electoral college for McClellan.

November 29, 1864 - While awaiting terms of surrender, Cheyenne and Arapaho Indians are raided by 900 cavalrymen at Sand Creek. Between 150-500 men, women, and children from the tribes died.

1865
April 1, 1865 - Major General Philip H. Sheridan, leading his forces of cavalry and infantry, battle to victory at Five Forks against Major General George E. Pickett. This battle southwest of Petersburg, Virginia, cuts the railroad supply line to Confederate troops. One day later, General Grant holds his final assault on Petersburg, forcing the evacuation of General Robert E. Lee.

April 9, 1865 - General Robert E. Lee, as commander in chief of Confederate forces, surrenders his 27,000 man army to Ulysses

S. Grant at Appomattox Court House, Virginia, effectively ending the four years of Civil War conflict. Additional troops under southern command would continue to surrender until May 26. The McLean House is the location for the surrender at Appomattox Courthouse.

April 14, 1865 - Abraham Lincoln is assassinated in Ford's Theatre, Washington, D.C.. five days after the signing at Appomattox of the Confederate surrender. The shot, fired by actor John Wilkes Booth, during the play "Our American Cousin," ends the life of the president who presided over the War of Rebellion and the end of slavery. Lincoln would die one day later.

June 28, 1865 - In the final desperate offensive act of the Civil War, two and one-half months after Lee's official surrender at Appomattox, the Confederate ship Shenandoah seized eleven American whaling ships in the Bering Strait, Alaska.

December 18, 1865 - The Thirteenth Amendment, abolishing slavery, takes effect.

1866
March 13, 1866 - The Civil Rights Act of 1866 is passed by Congress, the first federal law protecting the rights of African Americans. It is vetoed by President Johnson, but the veto overridden by Congress.

April 6, 1866 - The first post of the Grand Army of the Republic forms in Decatur, Illinois, and subsequently became a major political force. The G.A.R. began the celebration of Memorial Day in the north.

July 28, 1866 - Weights and measures are standardized in the United States when the Metric Act of 1866 passes Congress.

November 6, 1866 - The final Congressional elections of the year and election of additional Republicans lead to southern reconstruction being taken over by the federal government and freedman's rights backed.

December 24, 1866 - The Klu Klux Klan forms secretly to discourage blacks from voting, issuing in a brutal and shameful era of terror and crime amid southern states as civil rights for freed slaves emerged from the Civil War Era and made hesitant progress throughout the majority of the 20th Century.

1867
March 30, 1867 - Secretary of State William H. Seward consummates the sale of Alaska to the United States from Russia for $7.2 million dollars, approximately two cents per acre, by signing the Treaty of Cession of Russian America to the United States.

June 6, 1867 - The first running of the Belmont Stakes occurs at Jerome Park race track. The race was won by filly Ruthless at 1 5/8 mile with a winning purse of $1,850. The Belmont Stakes is the oldest of the three American Triple Crown races.

January 1867 - First of twelve installments of Ragged Dick by Horatio Alger is published and one year later expanded into a book in the "rags to riches" theme.

December 4, 1867 - The Grange organizes to protect the interest of the American farmer.

Christopher Sholes, Carlos Glidden, and S.W. Soule' invent the first practical typewriter. One year later, it was patented, then placed on the market in 1874 by E. Remington and Sons.

1868
March 5, 1868 - George Westinghouse invents and patents the air brake for railroad trains and organizes a company to produce them. Westinghouse would go on to patent four hundred inventions and found sixty companies, including Westinghouse Electric Company.

March 5, 1868 - The impeachment trial of Andrew Johnson begins in the Senate. Johnson was charged with violating the Tenure of Office Act by trying to remove the Secretary of War, Edwin M. Stanton. The President is acquitted by one vote.

October 28, 1868 - Thomas Edison applies for his first patent for the electric vote recorder.

November 3, 1868 - Republican Ulysses S. Grant, with Shuyler Colfax as his running mate, proves victorious in his quest to become the 18th President of the United States after defeating Horatio Seymour, 214 to 80 in the Electoral College. Grant would be sworn in on March 4, 1869.

November 27, 1868 - The Battle of the Washita River ends with Lt. Colonel George Custor's defeat of Black Kettle's Cheyenne. This ended the organized campaign of Indian forces against white settlers.

1869
May 10, 1869 - At Promontory, Utah, the final golden spike of the transcontinental railroad is driven into the ground, marking the junction of the Central Pacific and Union Pacific Railroads. This act, as much as any other, would signal the marked increase in the settlement of the west.

June 15, 1869 - John W. Hyatt, a New York printer, invents and patents celluloid, the first synthetic plastic used widely for commercial applications, including combs, dentures, curtains, and photographic film, as well as the billiard balls he was seeking to find a substitute for the ivory commonly used.

August 15, 1869 - The first scientific expedition of the Grand Canyon of the Colorado River is conducted by Major John Wesley Powell.

September 24, 1869 - Prompted by an attempt to corner the gold market, the financial Black Friday occurs in New York City.

December 10, 1869 - In one of the first acts of success in the women's suffrage movement, a Women's Suffrage law passes in the Territory of Wyoming.

1870

January 10, 1870 - Standard Oil Company is incorporated by John D. Rockefeller.

February 25, 1870 - The first African-American to be sworn into office in the United States Congress, Hiram Rhodes Revels, a Republican from Missouri takes his place in the United States Senate.

March 30, 1870 - The 15th Amendment to the Constitution is declared ratified by the Secretary of State. It gave the right to vote to black Americans. Race would officially no longer be a ban to voting rights.

June 1, 1870 - The 1870 census indicates a national population of 38,558,371, an increase in the United States count of 22.6% over the 1860 census. This lower than normal increase of population in the 1800's shows the effect of the national strife of the Civil War and the tragic losses during that campaign. The geographic center of the U.S. population, for the second decade in a row, is in Ohio, 48 miles east by north of Cincinnati.

July 15, 1870 - The last former state of the Confederacy, Georgia, is readmitted into the Union, and the Confederated States of America is officially dissolved.

November 1, 1870 - The National Weather Service, known as the Weather Bureau, makes its first official meteorological forecast. "High winds at Chicago and Milwaukee... and along the Lakes."

1871

January 17, 1871 - Andrew Smith Hallidie patents an improvement in endless wire and rope ways for cable cars. Regular service on the Clay Street Hill cable railway in San Francisco would begin September 1, 1873.

April 4, 1871 - The first professional baseball league, the National Association, debuts with a game between the Cleveland Forest

Citys and the Fort Wayne Kekiongas. Fort Wayne won the initial official game 2 to 0.

October 8, 1871 - The great fire of Chicago starts, in legend by a kick from Mrs. O'Leary's cow, although in actuality likely started in their cowshed by Daniel Sullivan who first reported the fire. The fire caused $196 million in damages. It burned 1.2 million acres of land, destroyed 17,450 buildings, killed 250 people, and left 90,000 homeless. Starting on the same day as the Chicago fire and overshadowed by its legend, a fire in Peshtigo, Wisconsin spreads across six counties in one day, and kills 1,200 to 2,500 people, making it the deadliest fire in United States history

October 27, 1871 - New York Mayor Boss Tweed is arrested. Thomas Nast, German-American caricaturist, who had skewed the Boss Tweed ring in his cartoons, is credited with an important role in his downfall.

November 17, 1871 - The National Rifle Association is granted a charter by the State of New York.

1872
February 20, 1872 - In New York, the Metropolitan Museum of Art opens.

March 1, 1872 - The world's first national park is established when President Grant signs legislation enabling the establishment of Yellowstone National Park in the states of Wyoming, Montana, and Idaho.

May 22, 1872 - Civil rights are restored to citizens of the South, except for five hundred Confederate leaders, with the passage of the Amnesty Act of 1872 and its signing by President Ulysses S. Grant.

October 21, 1872 - Kaiser Wilhelm I of Germany arbitrates the international boundary dispute, the Pig War, between the United States and Great Britain over the ownership of the straits between Washington Territory and Vancouver Island. He rules that San Juan Island is the property of the United States, ending twelve years of occupation by both armies.

November 5, 1872 - Susan B. Anthony, women's suffragette, illegally casts a ballot at Rochester, New York in the presidential election to publicize the cause of a woman's right to vote. The reelection of Republican President Ulysses S. Grant is granted by a landslide Electoral College victory, with 286 cast for Grant. His opponent, Horace Greeley, had died prior to the Electoral College vote, on November 29. His votes were split among four individuals.

1873
July 21, 1873 - Jesse James and the James-Younger Gang engage in the first successful train robbery in the American West, taking three thousand dollars from the Rock Island Express at Adair, Iowa.

August 4, 1873 - The Seventh Cavalry under the command of Lt. Colonel George Armstrong Custer, protecting a railroad survey party in Montana, engage the Sioux for the first time near the Tongue River in one minor clash of the Indian War. The Indian Wars, which had raged throughout 1873, saw the First Battle of the Stronghold on January 17, and the Second Battle of the Stronghold on April 15-17, and the end of the Modoc War on June 4 when Captain Jack was captured.

May 23, 1873 - The first running of the Preakness Stakes horse race, second in the leg of today's Triple Crown, debuts in Baltimore, Maryland in front of a crowd of 12,000. The horse, Survivor, owned by John Chamberlain, won by ten lengths over six other horses in a time of 2:43, winning a victor's purse of $1,850.

September 18, 1873 - An economic depression begins when the New York stock market crashed, setting off a financial panic that caused bank failures. The impact of the depression would continue for five years.

December 15, 1873 - The Women's Crusade of 1873-74 is started when women in Fredonia, New York march against retail liquor dealers, leading to the creation of the Woman's Christian Temperance Union. In 1917, this movement would culminate in the 18th Amendment, prohibiting the sale of liquor in the United

States, a ban that would last for sixteen years.

1874
January 1, 1874 - The Bronx is annexed by New York City.

March 18, 1874 - The island of Hawaii signs a trade treaty with the United States government granting it exclusive trading rights.

July 1, 1874 - The first United States zoo opens in Fairmount Park, Philadelphia.

November 7, 1874 - The debut of the symbol of the Republican Party, the elephant, occurs when Thomas Nast prints a cartoon utilizing the symbol in Harper's Weekly.

November, 25, 1874 - The U.S. Greenback Party is organized as a political organization by farmers who had been hurt financially in the Panic of 1873.

1875
March 1, 1875 - The Civil Rights Act, giving equal rights to blacks in jury duty and accommodation, is passed by the United States Congress. It would be overturned in 1883 by the U.S. Supreme Court.

March 15, 1875 - The first cardinal in the United States is named by the papacy, John McCloskey, the New York archbishop.

May 17, 1875 - The first Kentucky Derby is run at Churchill Downs in Louisville, Kentucky. It would become the first leg of today's Triple Crown Series. The horse Aristides is the first winner.

November 9, 1875 - Reporting on the Indian Wars, inspector E.C. Watkins pronounces that hundreds of Sioux and Cheyenne under Indian leaders Sitting Bull and Crazy Horse are openly hostile against the United States government, forming U.S. policy over the next year that would lead to battles such as Little Big Horn.

December 4, 1875 - New York City politician Boss Tweed escapes from prison and migrates to Cuba, then Spain. He would be captured and returned to New York authorities on November 23, 1876.

1876

January 31, 1876 - Original date issued by the United States government ordering all Native Americans onto a system of reservations throughout the western lands of the United States. Although the date would be extended by President Grant, this issue would lead to the Great Sioux War of 1876.

May 10, 1876 - The Philadelphia Centennial Exhibition, a world's fair meant to celebrate the 100th birthday of the United States opens on 285 acres in Fairmount Park, Philadelphia. Among its notable public showings include Alexander Graham Bell, with his newly patented telephone, Thomas Edison with the megaphone and phonograph, Westinghouse with the air brake, the first public showing of the top portion of the Statue of Liberty and the Corliss Engine, a steam engine so large it powered the entire exhibition and proved to the 34 nations and 20 colonies who exhibited that not only was the U.S.A. an equal on a par with European nations in manufactured goods, but had surpassed them in innovation.

June 25-26, 1876 - The Battle of Little Big Horn occurs when Lt. Colonel George Custer and his 7th U.S. Cavalry engage the Sioux and Cheyenne Indians on the bluffs above the Little Big Horn River. All 264 members of the 7th Cavalry and Custer perish in the battle, the most complete rout in American military history.

August 2, 1876 - Legislation is approved for the federal government to complete the privately sponsored, until that time, Washington Monument with an appropriation of $2 million.

November 7, 1876 - Samuel J. Tilden, Democrat, outpolls Rutherford B. Hayes, Republican in the popular vote, but reverses the outcome in the Electoral College by one vote. The presidential election, however, would not be decided until March 2, 1877, when disputed votes in four states (Florida, Louisiana, Oregon, and South Carolina) force Congress to declare Hayes the victor, in large part after Republicans agree to end reconstruction in the South.

November 10, 1876 - The Philadelphia Centennial Exhibition closes its exposition period after 159 days, not including Sundays, with a paid and free attendance of 8,095,349. Over 9.9 million people, including staff, saw the first large scale world's fair in the United States jump the United States into the upper echelon of nations with its exhibits and inventions. This exhibition was also credited with healing many of the wounds still left by the Civil War, binding the nation together with the effort.

1877
March 2, 1877 - A joint session of the U.S. Congress convenes on the presidential election dispute, reaching the Compromise of 1877 and electing Rutherford B. Hayes as President and William A. Wheeler as Vice President. They would be inaugurated two days later on March 4. Hayes would appoint Carl Schurz Secretary of the Interior, who began efforts to prevent forest destruction.

May 6, 1877 - Indian leader of the Oglala Sioux, Crazy Horse, surrenders to the United States Army in Nebraska. His people had been weakened by cold and hunger.

June 21, 1877 - The Molly Maguires, an Irish terrorist society in the minefields surrounding Scranton, Pennsylvania is broken up when eleven leaders are hung for murders of police and mine officials.

June 17, 1877 - The Nez Perce War begins when Nez Perce Indians route two companies of United States Army cavalry in Idaho Territory near White Bird. This is the first battle of the war. On August 9 Colonel John Gibbon commands the 7th U.S. Infantry as they clash with Nez Perce Indians at the Battle of the Little Big Hole. This war was fought when the Nez Perce tribe attempted to avoid confinement within the reservation system.

September 1, 1877 - Frederick Douglass, the ex-slave civil rights leader and abolitionist moved into his house, Cedar Hill, in the Anacostia section of Washington, D.C.

1878
January 6, 1878 - American poet, Carl Sandburg, is born. He would win two Pulitzer prizes for poetry and one for his biography

of Abraham Lincoln.

January 28, 1878 - In New Haven, Connecticut, the first commercial telephone exchange is opened.

February 18, 1878 - The Lincoln County War begins in New Mexico between two groups of wealthy businessmen, the ranchers and the Lincoln County general store. William Bonney, aka Billy the Kid, fought alongside the ranchers in a dispute over seizure of horses as a payment of an outstanding debt.

February 19, 1878 - Thomas Edison patents the cylinder phonograph or tin foil phonograph.

October 15, 1878 - The Edison Electric Company begins operation.

1879
February 15, 1879 - President Rutherford B. Hayes signs a bill that allowed female attorneys to argue in Supreme Court cases.

February 22, 1879 - The first five and dime store is opened in Utica, New York by Frank W. Woolworth with $300 of borrowed money, priced all items at five cents and pioneered the concept of fixed prices vs. haggling. It would fail weeks later. Woolworth, along with his brother Charles Sumner Woolworth, opened a second store in Lancaster, Pennsylvania in April 1879, including ten cent items, making the second store a success. By their 1911 incorporation, they had 586 stores.

March 14, 1879 - Albert Einstein, who would later revolutionize modern Physics, is born in Germany.

May 30, 1879 - The Gilmores Garden in New York City is renamed Madison Square Garden by William Henry Vanderbilt and opens to the public at 26th Street and Madison Avenue.

September 1879 - Henry George advocates a single tax on land in his publication, "Progress and Poverty."

1880
January 1, 1880 - The construction of the Panama Canal begins under French auspices, although it would eventually fail on the sea level canal in 1893, and would be bought out by the United States twenty-four years later under President Theodore Roosevelt.

June 1, 1880 - The national population in 1880 reached 50,189,209 people, an increase of 30.2% over the 1870 census. The geographic center of the U.S. population now reaches west/southwest of Cincinnati, Ohio in Kentucky. Five states now have more than two million in population; New York, Pennsylvania, Ohio, Illinois, and Missouri.

June 7, 1880 - The Yorktown Column, now part of Colonial National Historical Park in Virginia, is commissioned by the United States Congress. Its construction would commemorate the victory of American forces in the Revolutionary War.

October 23, 1880 - Adolph F. Bandelier enters Frijoles Canyon, New Mexico, under the guidance of Cochiti Indians and witnesses the prehistoric villages and cliff dwellings of the national monument that is named after him.

November 2, 1880 - James A. Garfield, Republican is elected president over Winfield S. Hancock, the Democratic candidate. Garfield receives 214 Electoral College votes to 155 for Hancock, but barely wins the popular vote with a majority of only 7,023 voters.

1881
January 25, 1881 - Thomas Edison and Alexander Graham Bell form the Oriental Telephone Company.

May 21, 1881 - The American Red Cross names Clara Barton president, a post she would hold until 1904 through nineteen relief missions.

July 2, 1881 - The 20th President of the United States, James A. Garfield, is shot by lawyer Charles J. Guiteau in the Baltimore and Potomac Railroad station in Washington, D.C. He would die two months later on September 19, 1881 from an infection and be succeeded in the presidency by Vice President Chester Arthur on September 20.

July 4, 1881 - The Tuskegee Institute for black students training to be teachers opens under the tutelage of Booker T. Washington as instructor in Tuskegee, Alabama.

July 20, 1881 - Sioux chief Sitting Bull leads the final group of his tribe, still fugitive from the reservation, and surrenders to United States troops at Fort Buford, Montana.

October 26, 1881 - The gunfight at the O.K. Corral in Tombstone, Arizona occurs in a livery stable lot between some of the famous characters of the American west; Sheriff Wyatt Earp, his brother Virgil, and Doc Holliday against Billy Claiborne, Frank and Tom McLaury and the Clanton brothers Billy and Ike. Although only thirty seconds long, the battle would live in western lore for more than one hundred years. The McLaury brothers and Billy Clanton would perish in the fight.

1882
January 2, 1882 - The Standard Oil Company trust of John D. Rockefeller is begun when Rockefeller places his oil holdings inside it.

January 30, 1882 - Future president Franklin Delano Roosevelt is born at his home in Hyde Park, New York.

February 7, 1882 - The final bare knuckle fight for the heavyweight championship is fought in Mississippi City.

March 22, 1882 - The practice of polygamy is outlawed by legislation in the United States Congress.

April 3, 1882 - Western outlaw Jesse James is shot to death by Robert Ford, a member of his own band, for a $5,000 reward. The Ford brothers had been recruited to rob the Platte City Bank, but opted to try to collect the reward for their infamous leader.

1883

January 16, 1883 - The Pendleton Civil Service Reform Act is passed by Congress, overhauling federal civil service and establishing the U.S. Civil Service agency.

February 28, 1883 - Vaudeville, the entertainment and theatrical phenomena, begins when the first theatre is opened in Boston, Massachusetts.

May 24, 1883 - The Brooklyn Bridge is opened. It was constructed under a design by German-American Johann A. Roebling and required fourteen years to build. Six days later, a stampede of people fearing a rumor about its impending collapse causes twelve people to be killed.

October 15, 1883 - The U.S. Supreme Court finds part of the Civil Rights Act of 1875 unconstitutional, allowing individuals and corporations to discriminate based on race.

November 18, 1883 - Five standard time zones are established by the United States and Canadian railroad companies to end the confusion over thousands of local time zones.

1884

May 1, 1884 - The Federation of Organized Trades and Labor Unions in the U.S.A. call for an eight-hour workday.

October 6, 1884 - The U.S. Naval War College is founded in Newport, Rhode Island.

October 23, 1884 - The first post season games in baseball were held between the National League champions, the Providence Grays, and the American Association champions, the New York Metropolitans. Providence would win the series, 3 games to 0.

November 4, 1884 - Grover Cleveland claims victory for the Democratic Party, gaining 277 Electoral College votes to the 182 Electoral College votes for the Republic candidate James G. Blaine.

December 6, 1884 - The capstone of three thousand three

hundred pounds is positioned atop the Washington Monument by the Corps of Engineers. The monument, five hundred and fifty-five feet tall and now completed after nearly thirty-seven years of work, would be dedicated in February of 1885.

1885
February 21, 1885 - The Washington Monument is dedicated at a ceremony by President Chester A. Arthur. The obelisk was completed under federal auspices after construction had been started by private concerns thirty-seven years earlier in 1848.

March 3, 1885 - American Telephone and Telegraph (ATT) is incorporated in New York City as a subsidiary of American Bell Telephone Company.

June 17, 1885 - The Statue of Liberty arrives for the first time in New York harbor.

July 23, 1885 - President Ulysses S. Grant, Civil War hero of federal forces, dies in Mt. McGregor, New York.

September 2, 1885 - The Rock Spring, Wyoming mining incident occurs when one hundred and fifty white miners attack Chinese coworkers, killing twenty-eight and forcing several hundred more to leave Rock Springs.

1886
January 20, 1886 - Thomas A. Edison buys Glenmont and builds a new laboratory for his experiments and inventions near West Orange, New Jersey. The home and grounds contain a 29 room Queen Anne mansion.

May 4, 1886 - The Haymarket riot and bombing occurs in Chicago, Illinois, three days after the start of a general strike in the United States that pushed for an eight hour workday. This act would be followed by additional labor battles for that worker right favored by unions. Later this year, on December 8, the American Federation of Labor (AFL) was formed by twenty-five craft unions.

May 8, 1886 - Dr. John Pemberton, a Georgia pharmacist, invents coca-cola, a carbonated beverage. On May 29,

Pemberton began to advertise Coca-Cola in the Atlanta Journal.

June 2, 1886 - President Grover Cleveland marries Francis Folsom in the White House Blue Room, the sole marriage of a president within the District of Columbia mansion during the history of the United States.

September 4, 1886 - At Fort Bowie in southeastern Arizona, Geronimo and his band of Apaches surrender to Brigadier General Nelson A. Miles. This signaled the end of warfare between the United States Army and Indian tribes.

October 28, 1886 - The Statue of Liberty, known during its construction and erection as "Bartholdi's Light" or "Liberty Enlightening the World" is dedicated by President Grover Cleveland in New York Harbor. First shown in the United States at the Centennial Exhibition in Philadelphia ten years earlier, the huge sculpture by French artist Auguste Bartholdi provided the beacon to millions of immigrants and citizens who would pass its position in the decades to come.

1887
January 20, 1887 - Pearl Harbor naval base is leased by the United States Navy, upon approval of the U.S. Senate.

January 21, 1887 - The Amateur Athletic Union (commonly referred to as the AAU) is formed. The association was created to assist teams and players in a variety of sports.

February 2, 1887 - The first Groundhog Day is observed in Punxsutawney, Pennsylvania, and the tradition of checking the shadow of a groundhog to predict the coming spring began.

October 22, 1887 - The statue of Abraham Lincoln, "Standing Lincoln," by Augustus Saint-Gaudens is unveiled in Lincoln Park, Chicago, Illinois.

November 8, 1887 - Naturalized as a citizen in 1881, Emile Berliner is granted a patent for the gramophone. Berliner, born in Hanover, Germany, had previously worked with Bell Telephone after selling his version of the microphone to the company.

1888

March 11-14, 1888 - The eastern section of the United States undergoes a great snow storm, killing four hundred people.

June 16, 1888 - The prototype for the commercial phonograph is completed by Thomas A. Edison and staff at his laboratory near Glenmont, his estate in West Orange, New Jersey.

October 8, 1888 - Work begins on the first motion picture camera at Thomas A. Edison's laboratory.

October 9, 1888 - The Washington Monument officially opens to the general public.

November 6, 1888 - Benjamin Harrison halts the goal of Grover Cleveland to be a two term president, for the time being. Harrison loses the popular vote to Cleveland, but wins the plurality of Electoral College electors, 233 to 168.

1889

March 2, 1889 - Legislation signed by President Grover Cleveland sets aside the first public lands protecting prehistoric features at the Casa Grande ruin in Arizona Territory. These lands could not be settled or sold.

March 23, 1889 - President Benjamin Harrison opens up Oklahoma lands to white settlement, beginning April 22, when the first of five land runs in the Oklahoma land rush start. More than 50,000 people waited at the starting line to race for one hundred and sixty acre parcels.

May 31, 1889 - The deadliest flood in American history occurs in Johnstown, Pennsylvania when 2,200 people perish from the water of the South Fork Dam after heavy rains cause its destruction.

June 3, 1889 - Running between the Willamette Falls and Portland, Oregon, a distance of fourteen miles, the first long distance electric power transmission line in the United States is completed.

July 8, 1889 - The first issue of the Wall Street Journal is published.

1890

September 27, 1890 - Rock Creek Park in Washington, D.C. is created when President Benjamin Harrison signs legislation creating natural preservation in the wooded valley within urban District of Columbia.

December 13, 1890 - Wilbur and Orville Wright print the "Dayton Tattler" in their print shop in Dayton, Ohio. The paper was the creation of Paul Laurence Dunbar, an African American poet.

December 29, 1890 - The Battle of Wounded Knee, South Dakota, occurs in the last major battle between United States troops and Indians. Hundreds of Indian men, women, and children are slain, along with twenty-nine soldiers.

June 1, 1890 - Preparations for the United States census begin using an automated tabulating machine with punch cards invented by Herman Hollerith. It was a historic moment in the history of computing; Hollerith's company eventually became IBM.

June 2, 1890 - The 1890 census indicates a population in the United States of 62,979,766, an increase of 25.5% since the 1880 census. Twenty miles east of Columbus, Indiana is now the geographic center of U.S. population.

1891

March 3, 1891 - The 51st Congress of the United States passes the International Copyright Act of 1891.

April 1, 1891 - The Wrigley Company is founded in Chicago, Illinois, originally selling soap, baking powder, and the next year, chewing gum.

May 5, 1891 - Carnegie Hall, then known as Music Hall, opens its doors in New York with its first public performance under the guest conductor, Tchaikovsky.

May 20, 1891 - The first showing to a public audience, the convention of the National Federation of Women's Clubs, of

Thomas A. Edison's new strip motion picture film occurred at Edison's West Orange, New Jersey laboratory. Later that year, Thomas Edison would patent the radio.

June 21, 1891 - Alternating current is transmitted for the first time by the Ames power plant near Telluride, Colorado by Lucien and Paul Nunn.

1892
January 1, 1892 - Ellis Island, in New York Harbor, opens as the main east coast immigration center, and would remain the initial debarkation point for European immigrants into the United States until its closure in 1954. More than 12 million immigrants would be processed on the island during those years. Ellis Island replaced Castle Garden, in Manhattan, as the New York immigration center.

January 15, 1892 - James Naismith publishes the rules of basketball and the first official game of basketball is held five days later at the YMCA in Springfield, Massachusetts.

April 15, 1892 - The General Electric Company is formed, merging the Edison General Electric Company with the Thomson-Houston Company.

October 12, 1892 - The first recital of the Pledge of Allegiance in U.S. public schools is done to mark the 400th anniversary of Columbus Day.

November 8, 1892 - Grover Cleveland returns to the presidency with his victory in the presidential election over incumbent President Benjamin Harrison and People's Party candidate James Weaver. Weaver, who would receive over 1 million votes and 22 Electoral College votes, helped defeat Harrison, who garnered only 145 Electoral College votes to Cleveland's 277.

1893
January 14-17, 1893 - The United States Marines, under the direction of U.S. government minister John L. Stevens, but no authority from the U.S. Congress, intervene in the affairs of the independent Kingdom of Hawaii, which culminated in the overthrow of the government of Hawaiian Queen Liliuokalani.

May 1, 1893 - The 1893 Chicago World Columbian Exposition, held on 686 acres and known affectionately as the White City, opens to the public. The world's fair hosted fifty nations and twenty-six colonies. Known today as the architectural wonder that saw replication of the styles of its white buildings throughout the United States in many public buildings for years to come, as well as the public initiation to the Ferris Wheel, a behemoth construction that held up to 2,160 riders.

May 5, 1893 - The New York Stock Exchange collapses, starting the financial panic of 1893. It would lead to a four year period of depression.

September 16, 1893 - The fourth of five land runs in Oklahoma's dash, known as the Oklahoma Land Race or the Cherokee Strip Land Run, opened seven million acres of the Cherokee Strip. It was purchased from the Indian tribe for $7,000,000. Nearly 100,000 people gathered around the 42,000 claims that were available to the first person, with a certificate, to stake a claim.

October 30, 1893 - The Chicago World's Fair closes after 179 days of public admission and over 25 million in attendance. It cost $27,291,715 and included a moving sidewalk and the first sighting of picture postcards. Considered by many historians as the greatest national event in American history through the year 1900.

November 7, 1893 - Women in Colorado are granted the right to vote.

1894
April 14, 1894 - The first public showing of Thomas Edison's kinetoscope motion picture is held. Edison had invented the process seven years earlier.

April 29, 1894 - In a march of five hundred unemployed workers into Washington, D.C. that had begun on March 25 in Massillon, Ohio, leader James S. Coxey is arrested for treason.

May 11, 1894 - A wildcat strike of three thousand Pullman Palace Car Company factory workers occurs in Illinois.

September 7, 1894 - The fight between heavyweight boxing champ Gentleman Jim Corbett and Peter Courtney is caught on motion picture film by Thomas Edison at the Black Maria studio of his New Jersey laboratory.

December 27, 1894 - Shiloh National Military Park in Shiloh, Tennessee is created to commemorate the field of the two day battle in April of 1862. It was one of the largest engagements between Union and Confederate forces in the western theatre of the U.S. Civil War.

1895
February 20, 1895 - Frederick Douglass, the ex-slave who rose to prominence in national politics as a civil rights advocate and abolitionist during Civil War times died at his home in Washington, D.C.

September 3, 1895 - The first professional football game is played in Latrobe, Pennsylvania. The Latrobe YMCA defeated the Jeannette Athletic Club 12-0.

October 4, 1895 - The first United States Golf Open run by the USGA is held in Newport, Rhode Island. A thirty-six hole competition between ten professionals and one amateur, the winner was Englishman Horace Rawlins, who received prize money of $150.

November 5, 1895 - The first United States patent for the automobile, #549160, is granted to George B. Selden for his two stroke automobile engine.

November 25, 1895 - Oscar Hammerstein opens the first theatre, Olympia, in the Times Square section of New York City.

1896
May 18, 1896 - Plessy versus Ferguson decision by the Supreme Court states that racial segregation is approved under the "separate but equal" doctrine.

April 6-15, 1896 - The first modern Olympic Games is held in Athens, Greece. Thirteen nations participated, including the

United States of America. It was held in Panathinaiko Stadium and had originated from an 1894 congress organized by Pierre de Coubertin who established the International Olympic Committee.

June 11, 1896 - Funds are appropriated by legislation signed into law by President Grover Cleveland to acquire the house across from Ford's Theatre. This home was the location where Abraham Lincoln died from his wounds in the theatre assassination by John Wilkes Booth.

August 16, 1896 - Gold is discovered by Skookum Jim Mason, George Carmack and Dawson Charlie near Dawson, Canada, setting up the Klondike Gold Rush which would cause a boom in travel and gold fever from Seattle to prospector sites surrounding Skagway, Alaska.

November 3, 1896 - Republican William McKinley claims victory in the presidential election with a majority of Electoral College voters, 271 selected him over Democratic and People's Party candidate William J. Bryan with 176.

December 10, 1896 - The New York City Aquarium at Castle Clinton opens on the tip of Manhattan Island. Castle Clinton, or Castle Garden, had been previously utilized in many capacities during the history of New York City; as a fort, entertainment location, and immigrant depot.

1897
April 15, 1897 - Oil is discovered in Indian territory for the first time on land leased from the Osage tribe, leading to rapid population growth near Bartlesville, Oklahoma.

April 19, 1897 - The first Boston Marathon is run with fifteen runners, won by John McDermott.

April 27, 1897 - The tomb of Ulysses S. Grant is dedicated in New York City, twelve years after his death.

July 17, 1897 - The Klondike Gold Rush begins with the arrival of the first prospectors in Seattle. The Gold Rush would be chronicled beginning eight days later when Jack London sails to the Klondike and writes his tales.

September 1, 1897 - The era of the subway begins when the first underground public transportation in North America opens in Boston, Massachusetts.

1898
February 15, 1898 - The rallying cry, "Remember the Maine" is struck when the United States battleship Maine explodes and sinks under unknown causes in Havana Harbor, Cuba, killing two hundred and sixteen seamen. The sentiment becomes a rallying point during the coming Spanish-American War.

April 22, 1898 - The blockade of Cuba begins when the United States Navy aids independence forces within Cuba. Several days later, the U.S.A. declares war on Spain, backdating its declaration to April 20. On May 1, 1898, the United States Navy destroyed the Spanish fleet in the Philippines. On June 20, the U.S. would take Guam.

May 12, 1898 - San Juan, Puerto Rico is bombed by the American navy under the command of Rear Admiral William T. Sampson. Puerto Rico is overtaken by the United States between July 25 with its landing at Guanica Bay and August 12. These acts during the Spanish-American War would ultimately result in Spain deciding in December to cede lands, including Puerto Rico, to the United States.

July 7, 1898 - The United States annexes the independent republic of Hawaii.

December 10, 1898 - The Peace Treaty ending the Spanish-American War is signed in Paris. The Spanish government agrees to grant independence to Cuba and cede Puerto Rico, Guam, and the Philippines to the United States.

1899
February 4, 1899 - Filipino independence fighters under leader Emilio Aguinaldo begin a guerrilla war after failing to gain a grant of independence from the United States, which they had been fighting for from Spain since 1896.

February 14, 1899 - The United States Congress approves the use of voting machines in federal elections.

March 2, 1899 - Mount Rainier National Park is established in Washington State.

March 28, 1899 – August Anheuser Busch, Jr., founder of Anheuser-Busch brewery company, is born. Also born this year are Al Capone, January 17, and Fred Astaire, May 10.

September 6, 1899 - The Open Door Policy with China is declared by Secretary of State John Hay and the U.S. government in an attempt to open international markets and retain the integrity of China as a nation.

<u>U.S. Timeline: The 1900's - The World Begins to Fly</u>

1900
March 14, 1900 - The Gold Standard Act is ratified, placing the United States currency on the gold standard.

April 15, 1900 - One of the largest world's fairs in history opens to the public in Paris, France with the United States among 42 nations and 25 colonies to exhibit. This world's fair also included the second modern Olympic Games held within its 553 acre site and would draw over thirty-nine million paid visitors through its close on November 12.

June 1, 1900 - Carrie Nation continues her Temperance Movement to abolish the consumption of liquor when she demolishes twenty-five saloons in Medicine Lodge. Also, on this day the 1900 census was conducted. In the first census of the 20th century, the population of the United States rose to 76,212,168, a 21% increase since 1890. For the first time, all fifty entities that would become the fifty states are included after Hawaii had officially become a territory of the United States on February 22. The center of the United States population, geographically, is now six miles southeast of Columbus, Indiana.

September 8, 1900 - The Galveston, Texas hurricane, with winds of 135 miles an hour, kills 8,000 people. It remains the most deadly natural disaster in American history. It was not named, during that era, and would have been a Category 4 storm on the Saffir-Simpson scale today.

November 6, 1900 - President William McKinley wins his second term as president, this time with Theodore Roosevelt in the second spot on the ticket, again defeating William J. Bryan by an Electoral Margin of 292 to 155.

1901
January 10, 1901 - The first major oil discovery in Texas occurs near Spindletop in Beaumont.

January 28, 1901 - The American League of Major League Baseball declares itself a Major League after one season as a minor league stemming from the minor Western League in 1899.

The eight charter teams included the Baltimore Orioles, the Boston Americans, Chicago White Sox, Cleveland Blues, Detroit Tigers, Milwaukee Brewers, Philadelphia Athletics, and the Washington Senators. 1901 signified its initial year of competition as a major league, competing against the senior National circuit.

March 2, 1901 - The Platt amendment is passed by the United States Congress, which limited the autonomy of Cuba as a condition for American troop withdrawal. Cuba would become a U.S. protectorate on June 12.

May 1, 1901 - The Pan-American Exposition opens in Buffalo, New York with nineteen international participants on 342 acres. It would close November 2, 1901 with a disappointing attendance of just over 5 million paid visitors, harmed by the tragedy of September 6.

September 6, 1901 - President William H. McKinley is shot at the Pan-American Exposition in Buffalo, New York while shaking hands with fair visitors, following his speech at the event on President's Day the day before. Anarchist Leon Czolgosz is arrested for the crime. On September 14, Vice President Theodore Roosevelt is inaugurated as President upon the death of William McKinley from gunshot wounds sustained the week earlier.

1902
January 1, 1902 - The first Rose Bowl is held, pitting the college football squads of the University of Michigan and Stanford. Michigan won the initial contest 49-0. It would be fourteen years until the second game, in 1916, when Washington State defeated Brown.

January 28, 1902 - A ten million dollar gift from Andrew Carnegie leads to the formation of the Carnegie Institution in Washington, D.C.

April 2, 1902 - The first movie theatre in the United States opens in Los Angeles, California. It was known as the Electric Theatre.

May 20, 1902 - The island of Cuba gains independence from the United States.

July 17, 1902 - Willis Haviland Carrier, a native of Angola, New York, invents the air conditioner. He would patent the device on February 2, 1906 and his company would air condition such buildings as Madison Square Garden, The U.S Senate, and House of Representatives.

1903
January 18, 1903 - The first two-way wireless communication between Europe and the United States is accomplished by Guglielmo Marconi when he transmits a message from President Theodore Roosevelt to the King of England from a telegraph station in South Wellfleet, Massachusetts.

May 23, 1903 - The first direct primary system in the United States is begun in the state of Wisconsin.

August 1, 1903 - The first cross-country automobile trip in the United States is completed with arrival in New York. The trip had begun in San Francisco on May 23.

October 1, 1903 - The first modern World Series of Major League Baseball is held between the American and National Leagues after two years of bitter rivalry. It pitted the pennant winners of that year in a nine game series, with the National League winner, Pittsburgh, coming out on top 5-3 games over Boston.

November, 3, 1903 - With United States support after the Hay-Herran Treaty rejection by Columbia earlier in the year, Panama declares its independence from Columbia. The Panama government is recognized by President Theodore Roosevelt three days later and a canal treaty is signed on November 18, allowing the U.S. led construction of the canal.

December 17, 1903 - Inventors Wilbur and Orville Wright succeed in the first sustained and manned plane flight, taking the heavier-than-air machine through the winds of Kill Devil Hill, North Carolina, and man into an age of flight. The plane, mechanically propelled with a petroleum engine, flew 120 feet in 12 seconds, and later the same day, flew 852 feet in 59 seconds. They would patent the Airplane three years later on May 22,

1906.

1904
April 30, 1904 - The Louisiana Purchase Exposition opens. Renowned for its spectacular ivory buildings, the inventions of the ice cream cone, and the "Meet Me in St. Louis" song. The St. Louis exposition closed December 1 with over nineteen million visitors. It was held on 1,272 acres. The Summer Olympic Games of 1904 were also twinned with the fair and were the first Olympic Games held in the western hemisphere.

May 5, 1904 - Cy Young, of the Boston Americans, pitches the first perfect game against the Philadelphia Athletics in the modern era of Major League baseball.

October 3, 1904 - The Daytona Educational and Industrial Training School for Negro Girls is opened by Mary McLeod Bethune in Daytona, Florida. Bethune is regarded as a leading contributor to the education of African-American students in the early 20th century.

November 8, 1904 - Theodore Roosevelt wins his first election for President after serving three years in the office due to the death of William McKinley. He defeats Democratic candidate Alton B. Parker, 336 to 140 in the Electoral College vote.

November 24, 1904 - The first successful field tractor is invented by American Benjamin Holt, using a caterpillar track to spread the weight in heavy agricultural machinery.

1905
February 23, 1905 - Rotary Club of Businessmen is founded with the first chapter in Chicago, Illinois.

March 4, 1905 - President Theodore Roosevelt is inaugurated for his second term.

April 6, 1905 - In the ruling of Lochner vs. New York, the ten hour work day law and sixty hour work week law for bakers is overturned by the U.S. Supreme Court. Work rule laws are routinely overturned until the West Coast Hotel Company vs. Parrish case in 1937.

May 15, 1905 - The city of Las Vegas, Nevada is formed with the sale of one hundred and ten acres in the downtown area.

June 1, 1905 - The Lewis and Clark Centennial Exposition is opened in Portland, Oregon. The world's fair would host eighteen nations and three colonies, and close on October 15 with attendance of 1.7 million visiting its 402 acre site.

1906
April 18-19, 1906 - The San Francisco earthquake occurs, estimated at 7.8 on the Richter scale. Its proximity to the epicenter of the San Andreas Fault and the subsequent fire that followed the quake and aftershocks left 478 reported deaths, although estimates in the future peg that figure at nearly 3,000. Between $350-$400 million in damages were sustained.

March 31, 1906 - The Intercollegiate Athletic Association of the United States is formed to set rules for amateur sports in the United States at the urging of President Theodore Roosevelt. It would become the National Collegiate Athletic Association in 1910.

June 8, 1906 - President Theodore Roosevelt grants protection to Indian ruins and authorizes presidents to designate lands with historic and scientific features as national monuments. This act, now known as the Antiquities Act, which would be utilized by Roosevelt to expand the National Parks system over his term was utilized for the first time on September 24, 1906 with the proclamation of Devils Tower National Monument in Wyoming, an 865 foot volcanic column. On June 29, legislation by Congress would continue to expand the national park system when it establishes Mesa Verde National Park in Colorado, preserving the most notable prehistoric cliff dwellings in the United States of America.

June 30, 1906 - The Pure Food and Drug Act and the Meat Inspection Act is passed.

November 9, 1906 - The first official trip abroad by a United States president occurs when Theodore Roosevelt leaves for a trip to inspect the progress in the construction of the Panama Canal.

1907

January 23, 1907 - The first Native American Senator, Charles Curtis, from Kansas, takes office.

March 13, 1907 - Another financial crises occurs in the business community with the beginning of the Financial Panic and Depression of 1907.

September 7, 1907 - The RMS Lusitania, the largest ship at the time, is launched on its maiden voyage from London to New York. The ship would be sunk by a German U-boat in 1915 during World War I, costing 1,198 people their lives.

November 16, 1907 - The Oklahoma Territory and the Indian Territory are combined to form Oklahoma and are admitted into the Union as the 46th state.

December 16, 1907 - The United States Great White Fleet of sixteen battleships and twelve thousand men begin their first round the world cruise.

1908

January 1, 1908 - The tradition of dropping a ball in New York's Times Square to signal the beginning of the New Year is inaugurated.

January 9, 1908 - Muir Woods National Monument, named after conservationist John Muir, is added to the National Park System by a proclamation of President Theodore Roosevelt after the two hundred and ninety-five acres of coastal redwood forest is donated by William Kent. On January 11, Roosevelt would add the Grand Canyon Monument to the system. On January 16, 1908, President Theodore Roosevelt proclaimed the Pinnacle National Forest of rock formations and caves as Pinnacles National Monument. On February 7, 1908, he would continue the expansion of federally protected lands with Jewel Cave National Monument in southwest South Dakota.

May 14, 1908 - Technology moves forward as the first passenger flight on a plane occurs when Wilbur Wright escorts Charles W. Furnas in the Wright Flyer III at Huffman Prairie Flying Field in

Dayton, Ohio. On September 27, the first production Model T is built at the Ford plant in Detroit, Michigan.

October 9, 1908 - The U.S. Bureau of Public Roads completes an initial two mile macadam surface through Cumberland Gap with the Object Lesson Road, one of the first efforts to test a hardened road.

November 3, 1908 - William Howard Taft is elected President, 321 to 162 Electoral Votes, over Democratic candidate William Jennings Bryan, who had twice before been defeated for the office by William McKinley in 1896 and 1900.

1909
January 28, 1909 - The troops of the United States leave Cuba for the first time since the beginning of the Spanish-American War.

April 6, 1909 - Admiral Robert E. Peary, a Pennsylvania native, accompanied by four eskimos and a black man, Matthew Henson, arrives as the North Pole on their sixth attempt, establishing Camp Jesup. He had set sail for the pole nearly one year earlier on July 6, 1908.

May 30, 1909 - The National Conference of the Negro is conducted, leading to the formation of the National Association for the Advancement of Colored People, (NAACP).

June 1, 1909 - The Alaska-Yukon Pacific Exposition opens in Seattle, Washington. Attendance of 3,740,561, including free visitors, witness the world's fair held on 250 acres, including land of present-day Washington University.

July 12, 1909 - President William Howard Taft continues the designation of national monuments begun during the Roosevelt administration with the proclamation of Oregon Caves National Monument in southwest Oregon. On July 31, he continued the designations with the southwestern Utah lands known as Mukuntuweap that would become, ten years later, Zion National Park.

1910
February 8, 1910 - The Boy Scouts of America is founded.

April 15, 1910 - In census of 1910 counted a United States population of 92,228,496. The 21% increase since the last census was the same rate of increase that had occurred during the previous decade. The center of the United States population was now within the city confines of Bloomington, Indiana.

May 11, 1910 - The start of American domestic tourism occurs with the establishment of Glacier National Park in Montana. Spurred by the development of the Great Northern Railroad, this park helped begin the See America First campaign to encourage United States tourists before and during World War I to visit the western states and territories.

May 16, 1910 - The United States Bureau of Mines is authorized by an act of the United States Congress.

May 25, 1910 - The only flight taken together by Wilbur and Orville Wright occurs at Huffman Prairie Flying Field in Dayton, Ohio. Later that same year, on November 7, the first flight to carry freight would depart from Huffman and deliver its cargo to Columbus, Ohio.

1911
January 18, 1911 - In San Francisco harbor, Eugene B. Ely lands his plane on the deck of the USS Pennsylvania for the first landing of a plane on a ship.

May 15, 1911 - Standard Oil is declared an unreasonable monopoly by the United States Supreme Court and ordered dissolved under the powers of the Sherman Antitrust Act.

May 30, 1911 - The Indianapolis 500 auto race is run for the first time in Indianapolis, Indiana. The race is won by Ray Harroun in the Marmon Wasp.

August 8, 1911 - The law establishing the number of United States representatives at 435 is passed. It would go into effect in

1913 after the 1912 elections.

September 17, 1911 - Technology moves forward. The first transcontinental airline flight was begun in New York by C.P. Rodgers. It would complete its journey to Pasadena, California after numerous stops and 82 hours and 4 minutes in the air on November 5. On October 10, Henry Ford patents the Automotive Transmission, Patent #1,005,186.

1912
March 12, 1912 - The American Girl Guides, renamed the Girl Scouts one year later, is formed in Savannah, Georgia.

April 20, 1912 - Fenway Park in Boston opens.

June 6, 1912 - Mount Katmai in southwest Alaska erupts in one of the largest recorded volcanic expulsions in the history of the world. It was designated Katmai National Monument in 1918 as protection against future eruptions.

August 14, 1912 - The United States Marines are sent to action in Nicaragua due to its default on loans to the United States and its European allies.

November 5, 1912 - In the first election of a Democratic candidate since 1892, Woodrow Wilson overcame a three way race for the presidency when former President Teddy Roosevelt donned the nomination of the Progressive Party to tackle the election against Wilson and incumbent President and Republican William Howard Taft. This split caused the election of Wilson, who garnered 435 Electoral College votes to 88 for Roosevelt and only 8 for Taft.

1913
February 1, 1913 - Grand Central Terminal, the world's largest rail terminal, opens in New York City. It is the third station on that site; the original depot built in 1871 and upgraded in 1900.

February 3, 1913 - The 16th Amendment to the United States Constitution is ratified, allowing the Federal government treasury to impose an income tax. The 17th Amendment would be passed on April 8, which set the policy for direct election of U.S.

Senators.

July 3, 1913 - The 50th Anniversary of the Battle of Gettysburg commemorates the Civil War battle. It draws thousands of remaining veterans of the battle and their families to the site of the Gettysburg Address and the northernmost battle of the war.

October 10, 1913 - The construction of the Panama Canal comes to a close when President Woodrow Wilson begins the explosion of the Gamboa Dike.

December 1, 1913 - The first moving assembly line is introduced and adopted for mass production by the Ford Motor Company, allowing automobile construction time to decrease by almost 10 hours per vehicle.

December 23, 1913 - A major reform of the American financial and banking system occurs with the authorization of the U.S. Congress for the establishment of the Federal Reserve System.

1914
January 5, 1914 - Basic wage rates are increased by Ford Motor Company. Workers now would receive $5 per day for eight hours of work versus $2.40 per day for nine hours previously.

April 20, 1914 - Ludlow, Colorado Coalfield Massacre occurs when the Colorado National Guard attacked a tent colony of one thousand two hundred striking miners, killing twenty-four.

July 11, 1914 - Babe Ruth makes his major league debut.

August 4, 1914 - President Woodrow Wilson announces that the United States will stay officially neutral in the European conflict that would become World War I. World War I hostilities had begun on June 28 when the Archduke of Austria and his wife, Franz Ferdinand and Sophie were killed by a Serb nationalist in Sarajevo. Hostilities would begin on July 28 when Austro-Hungary declared war on Serbia for failing to meet conditions set after the assassinations.

November 3, 1914 - New York socialite Mary Phelps Jacob patents the Brassiere in the United States, which she had invented one year earlier.

1915
January 25, 1915 - Alexander Graham Bell and Thomas A. Watson conduct the first telephone conversation between New York and San Francisco.

January 26, 1915 - The establishment of Rocky Mountain National Park, containing majestic mountain spires rising 14,000 feet within the Colorado Rockies is signed into law by President Woodrow Wilson after legislation was passed in the U.S. Congress. Later that same year, on November 30, Wilson would also designate the site of Pueblo Indian cliff dwellings, dating back to the year 1200, as Walnut Canyon National Monument, in Arizona.

January 28, 1915 - The United States Coast Guard is established, replacing the responsibilities formerly entailed within the services and stations of the U.S. Life-Saving Services.

February 20, 1915 - The Panama-Pacific International Exposition in San Francisco opens, signaling the rebirth of the city after the destruction of the 1906 Earthquake and fire, with the theme on the opening of the Panama Canal. Forty nations and colonies would exhibit on its 625 acres, despite the tensions that existed due to the start of World War I. The 1915 San Francisco World's Fair remains one of the most spectacular events in world expo history, lasting 288 days, and hosting over 13 million visitors.

June 15, 1915 - At graduation ceremonies of the United States Military Academy, future general and president Dwight D. Eisenhower is commissioned into the army as a 2nd Lieutenant.

May 7, 1915 - The British ship Lusitania is sunk by a German U-boat submarine, causing 128 American passengers to be lost. Germany, although it warned of the pending crises to passengers, issued an apology to the United States and promised payments.

1916
March 8-9 - Pancho Villa raids Columbus, New Mexico and other border towns along the Mexican and United States lines with

1,500 troops, that would lead, on March 16, to General John J. Pershing entering Mexico in pursuit of Villa with the 7th and 10th U.S. cavalry. Wilson had authorized 12,000 troops to cross the border one day earlier.

July 17, 1916 - Financial aid to farmers is awarded by the passage of the Rural Credits Act. These payments would be further strengthened with the passage of a second bill, the Warehouse Act, on August 11.

August 4, 1916 - The United States purchases the Virgin Islands from Denmark for $25 million and would take possession of the islands on March 31 of the next year.

August 25, 1916 - The National Park Service is officially created when President Woodrow Wilson signed legislation from Congress with the mission to protect and preserve the natural lands, historic sites, and wildlife of the system for future generations.

November 7, 1916 - Woodrow Wilson won a second term as President with his election in the Electoral College, 277 to 254 over Republican candidate Charles E. Hughes.

1917
February 3, 1917 - The United States government cuts diplomatic ties with Germany. The Zimmerman Telegram is given to the United States by Britain on February 24, showing the offer by Germany to give Mexico back the southwest United States if they would declare war on the United States.

March 11, 1917 - The United States recognizes the government of elected Mexican president Venustiano Carranza.

April 6, 1917 - Four days after receiving the request from President Woodrow Wilson, the United States Congress declares war on Germany and join the allies in World War I.

June 26, 1917 - The first troops from the United States arrive in Europe to assist European allies in World War I. Troops engaged in World War I would include conscript soldiers authorized by the passage of the Conscription Act, the Selective Services Act, on

May 18, 1917. General John Pershing would be placed in command of the American Expeditionary Forces during the campaign.

December 18, 1917 - The 18th Amendment, advocating prohibition of alcoholic beverages throughout the United States, is sent to the states for passage by the United States Congress.

1918
March 19, 1918 - Time zones are officially established by an act of the United States Congress with daylight savings time to go into effect on March 31.

May 15, 1918 - Airmail service is begun by the United States Post Office Department with regular service between New York, Philadelphia, and Washington.

July 1918 - By the middle of 1918, the United States military forces had over one million troops in Europe fighting in World War I.

August 1918 - The influenza epidemic Spanish flu spans the globe, killing over twenty million worldwide and five hundred and forty-eight thousand people in the United States.

November 11, 1918 - Hostilities in World War I begin to end with the Austria-Hungary alliance for armistice with the allies on November 3. Armistice Day with Germany occurs when the Allies and the German nation sign an agreement in Compiegne, France. Woodrow Wilson would become the first U.S. President to travel to Europe while in office when he sails to attend the Paris Peace Conference on December 4.

1919
January 16, 1919 - With the state of Nevada becoming the 36th state to ratify the 18th Amendment to the Constitution, prohibition becomes the law of the land. It would remain illegal to consume and sell alcoholic beverages in the United States until passage of the 21st Amendment, repealing the 18th, on December 5, 1933.

February 26, 1919 - The first natural lands east of the Mississippi River are established as a national park in legislation signed into law by President Woodrow Wilson. The area, known as Lafayette National Park in Maine is located at Mount Desert Island and known since 1929 as Acadia National Park.

May 8, 1919 - A United States navy seaplane begins the first transatlantic flight, making stops in Newfoundland and the Azores before touching ground in continental Europe in Lisbon, Portugal on May 27.

June 28, 1919 - The Treaty of Versailles is signed, ending World War I.

October 9, 1919 - In the first major scandal in Major League Baseball, and to this day, the worst, nine players from the Chicago White Sox throw the World Series to the Cincinnati Reds. It is forever known as the Black Sox Scandal with players, such as immortal Shoeless Joe Jackson, banned from the game and Hall of Fame forever.

1920

January 1, 1920 - For the first time, the 1920 census indicates a population in the United States over 100 million people. The 15% increase since the last census now showed a count of 106,021,537. The geographic center of the United States population still remained in Indiana, eight miles south-southeast of Spencer, in Owen County.

January 10, 1920 - The League of Nations is established with the ratification of the Treaty of Versailles, ending the hostilities of the first World War. Nine days later the United States Senate votes against joining the League.

February 3, 1920 - The first performance of the play, Beyond the Horizon, is held. The play by Eugene O'Neill would win the first of his four Pulitzer Prizes.

August 18, 1920 - Women are given the right to vote when the 19th Amendment to the United States constitution grants universal women's suffrage. Also known as the Susan B. Anthony amendment, in recognition of her important campaign to win the right to vote.

September 17, 1920 - The American Professional Football League is formed in 1920 with Jim Thorpe as its president and eleven teams. It would change its name to the National Football League in 1922.

November 2, 1920 - A landslide victory for Warren G. Harding in both the Electoral College and popular vote returns the Republican Party to the White House. Harding gained over 16 million popular votes to Democratic candidate James M. Cox's 9 million and won the Electoral contest with a 404 to 127 landslide. This was the first election in which women had the right to vote.

1921

May 19, 1921 - A national quota system on the amount of incoming immigrants is established by the United States Congress in the Emergency Quota Act, curbing legal immigration.

July 2, 1921 - A Congressional resolution by both houses is signed by President Warren G. Harding, declaring peace in World War I hostilities with Germany, Austria, and Hungary. The treaties would be executed one month later.

July 10, 1921 - The proposal for a trail along the Allegheny Mountain ridges is put forward by regional planner Benton MacKaye. The trail, completed in 1937 and designated officially as the Appalachian National Scenic Trail in 1968, stretches from Maine to Georgia.

September 7-8, 1921 - The first Miss America pageant is held in Atlantic City, New Jersey. It is won by Margaret Gorman for the title of the Golden Mermaid trophy, later dubbed Miss America.

November 12, 1921 - The Limitation on Armaments Congress convenes in Washington, D.C.

1922
February 5, 1922 - Reader's Digest is founded and the first issue published by Dewitt and Lila Wallace.

February 6, 1922 - The Armaments Congress ends. It would lead to an agreement, the Five Power Disarmament Treaty, between the major world powers of the United Kingdom, France, Italy, Japan, and the United States, to limit naval construction, outlaw poison gas, restrict submarine attacks on merchant fleets and respect China's sovereignty.

April 7, 1922 - The Teapot Dome scandal begins when the U.S. Secretary of the Interior leases the Teapot Oil Reserves in Wyoming.

May 5, 1922 - Construction begins on Yankee Stadium in New York City, often dubbed the House that Ruth Built.

May 30, 1922 - The Lincoln Memorial, located on the opposite end of the National Mall from the Capitol building, is dedicated in Washington, D.C.

1923

January 23, 1923 - The 12th century Aztec Indian ruins in New Mexico are proclaimed as a National Monument by President Warren G. Harding, following in the footsteps of all presidents since Theodore Roosevelt. It is known as Aztec Ruins National Monument.

March 2, 1923 - Time Magazine is published for the first time.

April 4, 1923 - Warner Brothers Pictures is incorporated.

April 15, 1923 - The first sound on film motion picture Phonofilm is show in the Rivoli Theatre in New York City by Lee de Forest.

August 2, 1923 - President Warren G. Harding dies in office after becoming ill following a trip to Alaska, and is succeeded by his Vice President, Calvin Coolidge. Coolidge would oppose the League of Nations, but approved of the World Court.

1924

January 25, 1924 - The first Winter Olympic Games are held in the French Alps in Chamonix, France with sixteen nations sending athletes to participate, including the United States, which won four medals. Norway, with four gold and eighteen medals total had the most in both categories. The Winter Olympic Games have been held since this year, except during World War II.

February 14, 1924 - The IBM corporation is founded.

May 10, 1924 - J. Edgar Hoover is appointed to lead the Federal Bureau of Investigation.

June 2, 1924 - All Indians are designated citizens by legislation passed in the U.S. Congress and signed by President Calvin Coolidge. The Indian Citizenship Act granted this right to all Native Americans that had been born within the territory of the United States.

November 4, 1924 - Calvin Coolidge wins his first election as President, retaining the White House for the Republican Party over his Democratic foe, John W. Davis, and Progressive Party candidate Robert M. La Follette. The Electoral margin was 382 to 136 (Davis) to 13 (La Follette).

1925
January 5, 1925 - Nellie Tayloe Ross is inaugurated as the first woman governor of the United States in Wyoming. Miriam Ferguson is installed two weeks later as the second during a ceremony in Texas.

June 13, 1925 - Radiovision is born. The precursor to television is demonstrated by Charles Francis Jenkins when he transmits a 10 minute film of synchronized pictures and sound for five miles from Anacostia to Washington, D.C. to representatives of the United States government.

July 10, 1924 - The Scopes Trial or Monkey Trial begins and would later convict John T. Scopes of teaching Charles Darwin's evolutionary theory at a Dayton, Tennessee high school, which violated Tennessee law. He is fined $100 for the charge.

November 21, 1925 - Lava Beds National Monument in California is designated by President Calvin Coolidge. It was the site of a volcanic rock, natural fortress used by the Modoc Indians during the Modoc War of 1872-3.

November 28, 1925 - The Grand Ole Opry transmits its first radio broadcast.

1926
March 16, 1926 - Robert H. Goddard demonstrates the viability of the first liquid fueled rockets with his test in Auburn, Massachusetts. The rocket flew one hundred and eighty-four feet over 2.5 seconds.

May 9, 1926 - The first flight to the North Pole and back occurs when pilot Floyd Bennett, with Richard Evelyn Byrd as his navigator, guided a three-engine monoplane. They were awarded the Medal of Honor for their achievement.

May 20, 1926 - Air Commerce Act is passed, providing aid and assistance to the airline industry, plus federal oversight under the Department of Commerce for civil air safety.

May 31, 1926 - The Sesqui-Centennial Exposition opens in Philadelphia to celebrate the one hundred and fiftieth birthday of the United States. With nineteen nations and four colonies participating, the event failed to live up to the wonder and expectation of the former Centennial Exposition, and is often regarded as a failure in world expo circles. Due in part to inadequate preparation and a very wet summer, it closed on November 30 a disappointment with 6 million visitors in total attendance.

November 15, 1926 - The NBC Radio Network is formed by Westinghouse, General Electric, and RCA, opening with twenty-four stations.

1927
March 5, 1927 - The civil war in China prompts one thousand United States marines to land in order to protect property of United States interests.

April 22 to May 5, 1927 - The Great Mississippi Flood occurs, affecting over 700,000.

May 20, 1927 - Charles Lindbergh leaves Roosevelt Field, New York on the first non-stop transatlantic flight in history. He would reach Paris thirty-three and one-half hours later in the Spirit of St. Louis, his aircraft. A ticker tape parade would be held in New York City after his return on June 13.

October 4, 1927 - Work on the gigantic sculpture at Mount Rushmore begins. Sculptor Gutzon Borglum would complete the task of chiseling the busts of four presidents; George Washington, Thomas Jefferson, Abraham Lincoln, and Theodore Roosevelt, fourteen years later.

October 6, 1927 - The advent of talking pictures emerges. Al Jolson in the Jazz Singer debuts in New York City.

September 7, 1927 - First success in the invention of television occurs by American inventor Philo Taylor Farnsworth. The complete electronic television system would be patented three years later on August 26, 1930.

1928

March 26, 1928 - The Tennessee national military park known as Fort Donelson National Battlefield, site of the first major Union victory in the Civil War and known for the unconditional surrender of Confederate troops to Brigadier General Ulysses S. Grant, is created by legislation signed into law by President Calvin Coolidge.

May 15, 1928 - The first appearance of Mickey and Minnie Mouse on film occurs with the release of the animated short film, Plane Crazy.

June 17, 1928 - Amelia Earhart becomes the first woman to fly over the Atlantic Ocean.

November 6, 1928 - Herbert Hoover wins election as President of the United States with an Electoral College victory, 444 to 87 over Democratic candidate Alfred E. Smith, the Catholic governor of New York.

December 21, 1928 - The United States Congress approves the construction of Boulder, later named Hoover Dam.

1929

January 15, 1929 - Future Civil Rights leader Martin Luther King is born in his grandfather's house in Atlanta, Georgia.

February 14, 1929 - In Chicago, Illinois, gangsters working for Al Capone kill seven rivals and citizens in the act known as the St. Valentine's Day Massacre.

October 11, 1929 - JC Penney opens its Store #1252 in Milford, Delaware, the last state in the Union to have one of their stores. The growth of the nationwide chain indicated the prosperity of the decade only two weeks before the stock market crash of 1929 would ensue.

October 25, 1929 - The Teapot Dome scandal comes to a close when Albert B. Fall, the former Secretary of the Interior, is convicted of accepting a $100,000 bribe for leasing the Elk Hills naval oil reserve. He is sentenced to one year in jail and a $100,000 fine.

October 29, 1929 - Postwar prosperity ends in the 1929 Stock Market crash. The plummeting stock prices led to losses between 1929 and 1931 of an estimated $50 billion and started the worst American depression in the nation's history.

1930
February 18, 1930 - American astronomer Clyde Tombaugh
discovers the planet Pluto at the Lowell Observatory in Flagstaff,
Arizona. Tombaugh was also known as one of the few serious
astronomers to have claimed to sight UFO's.

April 1, 1930 - The population counted in the 1930 census
reaches 123,202,624, a 16.2% increase over the past decade.
The geographic center of the United States population had
reached three miles northeast of Linton in Greene County,
Indiana.

April 22, 1930 - The London Naval Reduction Treaty is signed
into law by the United States, Great Britain, Italy, France, and
Japan, to take effect on January 1, 1931. It would expire on
December 31, 1936.

June 17, 1930 - The Smoot-Hawley Tariff Act is signed by
President Herbert Hoover. Its effective rate hikes would slash
world trade.

August 12, 1930 - Technology moves forward. Clarence
Birdseye invents frozen food with his quick-freezing process and
patents the concept. Also in 1930, the analog computer, or
differential analyzer, is invented at the Massachusetts Institute of
Technology in Boston by Vannevar Bush. Bush is also
considered a pioneer in the development of the concept for the
World Wide Web, with his idea for the memex.

December 2, 1930 - In order to combat the growing depression,
President Herbert Hoover asks the U.S. Congress to pass a
$150 million public works project to increase employment and
economic activity. On the New York City docks, out of work men
wait for food and jobs during the Great Depression, an outcome
of the Stock Market crash of 1929 after the prosperous decade of
the 1920's.

1931
February 14, 1931 - The ruins of the ancient Indian villages
around Canyon de Chelly are designated a national monument

by President Herbert Hoover.

March 3, 1931 - The Star-Spangled Banner, by Francis Scott Key, is approved by President Hoover and Congress as the national anthem. The lyrics of the anthem were inspired during the bombing of Fort McHenry by British ships at the head of Baltimore harbor in September of 1814.

March 17, 1931 - The state of Nevada legalizes gambling.

May 1, 1931 - Construction is completed on the Empire State Building in New York City and it opens for business. On the same day in Aniakchak Caldera, Alaska, a major eruption of Half Cone occurred, blackening the skies in southwestern Alaska for the next several weeks.

October 4, 1931 - Cartoonist Chester Gould creates the debut appearance of the Dick Tracy comic strip.

1932
January 22, 1932 - The Reconstruction Finance Corporation is established to stimulate banking and business. Unemployment in 1932 reached twelve million workers.

January 23, 1932 - Carlsbad Caverns National Park installs and inaugurates the use of high speed elevators to descend visitors into the depths of the caves. These elevators travel seventy-five stories in one minute.

March 1, 1932 - The infant son of Charles Lindbergh and Anne Morrow Lindbergh, Charles Augustus Lindbergh, Jr., is kidnaped. He is found dead on May 12 not far from his home in Hopewell, New Jersey. Three years later, on February 13, 1935, Bruno Hauptmann was found guilty of the crime.

August 23, 1932 - The highest continuous paved road in the United States, the Trail Ridge Road in Rocky Mountain National Park, Colorado, is opened to traffic.

November 8, 1932 - Democratic challenger Franklin D. Roosevelt defeats incumbent President Hoover in the presidential election for his first of an unprecedented four terms. The landslide victory,

472 Electoral College votes to 59 for Hoover began the era of FDR that would lead the nation through the vestiges of the Great Depression and the ravages of World War II.

1933
March 4, 1933 - President Franklin D. Roosevelt is inaugurated for the first time. His speech with its hallmark phrase, "We have nothing to fear, but fear itself," begins to rally the public and Congress to deal with great depression issues. His subsequent Fireside Chats, that began eight days later, would continue his addresses with the American public.

March 9 - June 16, 1933 - The New Deal social and economic programs are passed by the United States Congress in a special one hundred day session to address depression era economics. The gold standard was dropped on April 19 and ratified during the time of this session on June 5. Canada also drops using the gold standard.

March 31, 1933 - The Civilian Conservation Corps is authorized under the Federal Unemployment Relief Act. It would provide work for two and one-half million men during the succeeding nine years and help construct many national park and other projects across the United States.

May 27, 1933 - The Century of Progress World's Fair opens in Chicago, Illinois. Held along the banks of Lake Michigan on 427 acres, this depression era fair was a successful event, both in financial and attendance terms, taking advantage of cheap labor to keep costs low. It lasted for two seasons, drawing over 39 million visitors over its 1933 and 1934 years.

November 11, 1933 - In South Dakota, a strong dust storm strips topsoil from depression era farms. It was one in a series of such storms to plague the Midwest during 1933 and 1934.

December 5, 1933 - The 21st Amendment to the U.S. Constitution is passed, ending prohibition.

1934
March 22, 1934 - The Master's golf tournament is held for the first time at Augusta National Golf Club, founded by the

legendary amateur golfer Bobby Jones, in Augusta, Georgia. The 1934 winner was Horton Smith, of the United States, at four under par.

June 6, 1934 - The U.S. Securities and Exchange Commission is established with the signing of the Securities Exchange Act into law by President Franklin D. Roosevelt.

June 19, 1934 - The construction of the Natchez Trace Parkway, a scenic and historic trail between Nashville, Tennessee, and Natchez, Mississippi is approved in legislation signed by President Franklin D. Roosevelt.

August 15, 1934 - The United States pulls its troops from Haiti.

December 29, 1934 - Japan renounces the Washington Naval Treaty of 1922 and the London Naval Treaty of 1930.

1935
January 4, 1935 - Franklin D. Roosevelt issues a presidential proclamation designating the Fort Jefferson National Monument, now Dry Tortugas National Park, off the Florida Keys. The waters and islands of this area contain the largest all-masonry fort in the Western hemisphere.

June 2, 1935 - The greatest hitter in the history of baseball, Babe Ruth, retires from Major League Baseball. He is among the charter class of players inducted into the Baseball Hall of Fame, in Cooperstown, New York, in 1939.

August 14, 1935 - The Social Security Act is passed by Congress as part of the New Deal legislation and signed into law by President Franklin D. Roosevelt. It would begin payouts to retirees within two years. Workers began contributing into the system during the same year, at a rate of 2% of the first $3,000 in earnings, half paid by the employee and half paid by the employer.

August 21, 1935 - The Historic Sites Act is signed into law by President Franklin D. Roosevelt, declaring a national policy to preserve historic sites, including National Historic Landmarks.

October 10, 1935 - Porgy and Bess, the opera by George Gershwin, opens in New York City.

September 30, 1935 - Hoover Dam is dedicated by President Roosevelt.

1936
March 19, 1936 - Located at the homestead of Daniel Freeman, a filer of one of the initial homestead applications under the Homestead Act of 1862, the Homestead National Monument in Nebraska is signed into law by President Franklin D. Roosevelt. This historic site pays tribute to the many pioneers who settled the western states.

May 12, 1936 - The Santa Fe Railroad inaugurates the all-Pullman Super Chief passenger train service between Chicago, Illinois and Los Angeles, California.

May 30, 1936 - Gone with the Wind is published by Margaret Mitchell.

August 1, 1936 - The Summer Olympics Games open in Berlin, Germany under the watchful eye of German leader Adolph Hitler, whose policies of Arian supremacy had already begun to take shape. The star of the games was Jesse Owens, a black American, who won four gold at the Berlin 1936 Games.

November 3, 1936 - Franklin D. Roosevelt overwhelms his Republican challenger, Alfred Landon, for a second presidential term. His Electoral College margin, 523 to 8, and 62% of the popular vote insured Roosevelt carte blanche in his goals of the New Deal.

1937
February 16, 1937 - Wallace H. Carothers patents the polymer, invented in the Dupont labs.

March 26, 1937 - William Henry Hastie is appointed to the federal bench, becoming the first African-American to become a federal judge.

May 6, 1937 - At Lakehurst, New Jersey, the German airship

Hindenburg bursts into flames while mooring. The fire consumes the largest airship in the world, 804 feet long, within one minute, causing the death of thirty-six people.

May 27, 1937 - The Golden Gate Bridge opens to pedestrian traffic and one day later, after a ceremonial press of a button from Washington, D.C. by President Roosevelt, receives its first vehicles. It created a vital link between San Francisco and Marin County.

August 14, 1937 - The Appalachian Trail, extending two thousand miles from Mount Katahdin, Maine to Springer Mountain, Georgia is completed.

1938
May 17, 1938 - The Naval Expansion Act passes.

June 25, 1938 - The National Minimum Wage is signed into law within the federal legislation known as the Fair Labor Standards Act. It established a minimum wage of $0.25 at the time, as well as time and one half for overtime and the prohibition of most employment for minors.

July 3, 1938 - The final reunion of the Blue and the Gray is held. It commemorated the 75th anniversary of the Battle of Gettysburg in Gettysburg, Pennsylvania.

July 18, 1938 - Wrong Way Douglas Corrigan, with his faulty compass, lands his plane in Dublin, Ireland after departing from Brooklyn, New York on a trip to the west coast of the United States.

October 30, 1938 - A nationwide scare develops when Orson Welles broadcasts his War of the Worlds radio drama, which included fake news bulletins stating that a Martian invasion had begun on earth.

1939
January 5, 1939 - President Franklin D. Roosevelt asks the U.S. Congress for a defense budget hike.

April 30, 1939 - The New York World's Fair opens for its two year run. This world's fair, spectacularly conceived for the Flushing Meadows trash dump made famous by F. Scott Fitzgerald in Queen's, New York, is often credited with proving to the American public that prosperity and good times could lay ahead after the decade of depression. The fair was centered by the Trylon and Perisphere theme structures and included the participation of 52 nations and 11 colonies, despite the growing presence of a looming World War. The New York fair closed on October 21, 1940 and drew 45 million paid visitors. During the same year, a competing fair in San Francisco, known as the Golden Gate Exposition, became a second example of a spectacular world's fair signaling the end of the depression era. Held in the middle of San Francisco Bay, it opened February 18, 1939 and would close on September 29, 1940 with an attendance of over 15 million.

June 12, 1939 - The Baseball Hall of Fame opens in Cooperstown, New York, home of one of baseball's founders, Abner Doubleday. The first class of inductees included Ty Cobb, Babe Ruth, Honus Wagner, Christy Mathewson, and Walter Johnson.

August 2, 1939 - Albert Einstein alerts Franklin D. Roosevelt to an A-bomb opportunity, which led to the creation of the Manhattan Project. Einstein had arrived as a fugitive from Nazi Germany six years earlier on October 17, 1933.

September 5, 1939 - The United States declares its neutrality in the European war after Germany invaded Poland, effectively beginning World War II after a year of European attempts to appease Hitler and the aims of expansionist Nazi Germany.

1940
April 1, 1940 - The 1940 census indicates a United States population of 132,164,569. This represented an increase of 7.3% since 1930, the lowest rate of increase in the 20th century. The center of the United States population was geographically placed two miles southeast by east of Carlisle, Indiana.

June 3, 1940 - The United States government approves a sale of surplus war material to Great Britain.

June 14, 1940 - On the same day Paris fell to the German army and Auschwitz received its first Polish prisoners, the Naval Expansion Act is signed into law by President Franklin D. Roosevelt, increasing the capacity of the U.S. Navy by 11%. Four days earlier, Roosevelt had condemned the actions of Italy's declaration of war against France and the United Kingdom.

September 2, 1940 - The Great Smoky Mountains National Park, the most visited park in the National Park Service today, is officially dedicated by President Franklin D. Roosevelt. The park, whose land had been acquired in part by John D. Rockefeller, Jr. with a $5 million contribution, straddles the North Carolina and Tennessee state lines.

September 16, 1940 - The U.S. Congress approves and enacts the first peacetime conscription draft.

November 5, 1940 - President Franklin D. Roosevelt continues his dominance of presidential politics with a 449 to 82 Electoral College victory over Republican candidate Wendell Wilkie, winning his third presidential election. Roosevelt becomes the first man to hold office for three terms.

1941
March 11, 1941 - The George Washington Carver Museum is dedicated at the Tuskegee Institute with the participation of such luminaries as Henry Ford. The museum is now part of the Tuskegee Institute National Historic Site.

March 11, 1941 - The Lend-Lease Act is approved, which

provided $7 billion in military credits for American manufactured war supplies to Great Britain and other allies; in the fall, a similar Lend-Lease pact would be approved for the USSR with a $1 billion loan.

July 7, 1941 - The United States occupies Iceland, taking over its defense from Great Britain and attempting to thwart a potential invasion by Nazi Germany.

August 14, 1941 - An eight point declaration of principles called the Atlantic Charter is issued by President Roosevelt and Great Britain Prime Minister Winston Churchill.

September 28, 1941 - Ted Williams ends the 1941 season with a batting average over 0.400, the last player to accomplish that feat.

December 7, 1941 - The attack on Pearl Harbor, Hawaii, commences at 7:55 a.m. when Japanese fighter planes launch a surprise attack on United States soil, destroying the U.S. Pacific Fleet docked at the base. This attack, which took the greatest amount of U.S. naval life in history with 1,177 sailor and marines perishing in the attack, as well as the loss or damage to twenty-one naval ships, led to the entry of American troops into World War II. One day later, the United States of America declares war on Japan, officially entering World War II. On December 11, 1941, the United States declares war on Germany and Italy, responding to their declaration of war against America.

1942
February 19, 1942 - Executive order 9066 is signed into law by President Franklin D. Roosevelt, confining 110,000 Japanese Americans, including 75,000 citizens, on the West Coast into relocation camps during World War II. The remains of the first of these detention camps resides in California's Manzanar National Historic Site. These camps would last for three years.

June 4-7, 1942 - The Battle of the Midway is fought at Midway Islands in the Pacific with the Japanese fleet encountering its first major defeat of the war against the United States military. As the Battle of Midway comes to an end on June 7, Japan invades the Aleutian Islands, the first invasion of American soil in 128 years.

June 20, 1942 - The development of the first atomic bomb is signed into agreement between the Prime Minister of Great Britain, Winston Churchill, and President Franklin D. Roosevelt in Hyde Park, New York.

August 7, 1942 - The United States Marines land on Guadalcanal in the Solomon Islands in the first American offensive of World War II. A naval battle would commence on November 12 for three days with the U.S. Navy able to retain control despite heavy losses.

November 8, 1942 - North Africa is invaded by the United States and Great Britain.

December 2, 1942 - The first nuclear chain reaction is produced at the University of Chicago in the Manhattan Project, creating fission of the Uranium U-235, under the direction of physicists Arthur Compton and Enrico Fermi.

1943
February 14, 1943 - The United States encounters its first major defeat in the European theater of World War II at the Battle for Kasserine Pass in Tunisia.

April 13, 1943 - The Jefferson Memorial in Washington, D.C. is dedicated on the 200th anniversary of Thomas Jefferson's birth by President Franklin D. Roosevelt.

June 21, 1943 - Race riots in Detroit and Harlem cause forty deaths and seven hundred injuries.

July 10, 1943 - The United States Army's 45th Infantry Division lands on the island of Sicily, starting the campaign of Allied invasion into Axis-controlled Europe. Nine days later, Rome is bombed by Allied forces. The conquest of Sicily would be completed on August 17 when U.S. forces under General Patton and British forces under Field Marshall Montgomery arrive.

November 28, 1943 - The Tehran Conference is held for three days, concluding in an agreement between U.S. President Franklin D. Roosevelt, British Prime Minister Winston Churchill, and Soviet leader Josef Stalin about a planned June 1944 invasion of Europe with the code name Operation Overlord.

1944
June 6, 1944 - The Normandy Invasion, D-Day, occurs when one hundred and fifty-five thousand Allied troops, including American forces and those of eleven other Allied nations (Australia, Belgium, Canada, Czechoslovakia, France, Greece, the Netherlands, New Zealand, Norway, Poland, and the United Kingdom) land in France. Allied soldiers stormed the beaches of France to begin the World War II invasion of Europe that would lead to the liberation of Paris. Operation Overlord gained footing quickly, pushing through the Atlantic Wall in the largest amphibious military operation in history.

June 22, 1944 - The G.I. Bill of Rights is signed into law, providing benefits to veterans.

July 17, 1944 - The greatest continental U.S. tragedy of World War II occurs when two ships loading ammunition at Port Chicago Naval Weapons Station in California explodes. The accident killed three hundred and twenty people.

July 21, 1944 - The United States military begins to retake the island of Guam after Japanese troops had occupied the island during World War II. The battle would end on August 10.

November 6, 1944 - The last campaign speech of Franklin D. Roosevelt, seeking his fourth term in office, is broadcast from his Hyde Park, New York home. One day later, Roosevelt would gain that fourth term by a significant, but smaller margin than any of his previous elections, especially in the popular vote where Dewey lost by only three and one half million votes. The Electoral College margin, however, at 432 to 99, insured Roosevelt good footing in prosecution of World War II.

December 18, 1944 - The United States Supreme Court rules in the case of Korematsu vs. the United States, the wartime internment of Japanese Americans on the West Coast was valid during a time of war.

1945

February 4-11, 1945 - President Roosevelt, Prime Minister Churchill, and Premier Josef Stalin hold the Yalta Conference in the Soviet Union.

February 19, 1945 - Thirty thousand United States Marines land on Iwo Jima. On April 1, American troops invade Okinawa, beginning the Battle of Okinawa, which would continue until June 21.

March 1, 1945 - American troops cross the Rhine River at Remagen, Germany. Two weeks later, on March 18, twelve hundred and fifty U.S. bombers attack Berlin, causing Adolf Hitler to announce the destruction of his own industries and military installations one day later.

April 12, 1945 - President Roosevelt dies suddenly; Vice President Harry S. Truman assumes the presidency and role as commander in chief of World War II.

May 7, 1945 - The unconditional surrender of Germany at Reims, France concludes the military engagements of World War II in Europe. It is accepted by General Dwight D. Eisenhower in his role as the commander of Allied troops in the European theater of the war.

July 16, 1945 - The first atomic bomb, the Trinity Test, is exploded at Alamogordo, New Mexico, after its production at Los Alamos.

August 6, 1945 - President Harry S. Truman gives the go-ahead for the use of the atomic bomb with the bombing of Hiroshima. Three days later, the second bomb is dropped on Nagasaki, Japan. On August 15, Emperor Hirohito of Japan surrenders.

1946
January 10, 1946 - The first meeting of the United Nations general assembly occurs after its founding on October 24, 1945 by fifty-one nations, including the Security Council nations of China, France, the Soviet Union, the United Kingdom, and the U.S.A. These actions would lead to the disbanding of the League of Nations on April 18, when its mission was transferred to the U.N.

April 1, 1946 - Four hundred thousand mine workers begin to strike, with other industries following their lead.

June 6, 1946 - The Basketball Association of America, known as the National Basketball Association (NBA) since 1949 after its merger with the rival National Basketball League, is founded.

July 4, 1946 - The island nation of the Philippines is given their independence by the United States. This ends four hundred and twenty-five years of dominance by the west.

August 1, 1946 - The Atomic Energy Commission is established.

1947
March 12, 1947 - The Truman Doctrine is announced to the U.S. Congress. When passed it would grant $400 million in aid to Greece and Turkey to battle Communist terrorism. President Harry S. Truman implements the act on May 22.

April 2, 1947 - The United Nations Security Council unanimously approves the trusteeship of Pacific Islands formerly controlled by Japan to the United States.

April 15, 1947 - Jackie Robinson breaks Major League Baseball's barrier against colored players when he debuts at first base for Branch Rickey's Brooklyn Dodgers.

April 25, 1947 - Theodore Roosevelt National Park is established by President Harry Truman along the Little Missouri River and scenic badlands of North Dakota.

June 5, 1947 - Secretary of State George C. Marshall proposes aid extension to European nations for war recovery, known as the Marshall Plan, which would lead to Congressional approval of $12 billion over the following four years.

June 20, 1947 - President Harry S. Truman vetoes the Taft-Hartley Labor Act that would have curbed strikes, only to be overridden by Congress on June 23.

1948

April 1, 1948 - The Soviet Union begins its land blockade of the Allied sectors of Berlin, Germany. A counter blockade by the west was put into effect, as well as a British and U.S. airlift of supplies and food, until both blockades were lifted on September 30, 1949.

April 30, 1948 - The Organization of American States is founded by twenty-one nations to provide a mutual security pact after World War II. Founding nations were Argentina, Bolivia, Brazil, Chile, Columbia, Costa Rica, Cuba, Dominican Republic, Ecuador, El Salvador, Guatemala, Haiti, Honduras, Mexico, Nicaragua, Panama, Paraguay, Peru, the United States, Uruguay, and Venezuela.

July 26, 1948 - Executive Order 9981, ending segregation in the United States military, is signed into effect by President Harry S. Truman.

November 2, 1948 - President Harry S. Truman rallies from behind, capturing his first president election from the supposed winner Thomas E. Dewey, the governor of New York. Headlines in national newspapers had overtly announced a Dewey victory, only to be proven wrong. Truman won the Electoral College vote with 303 to Dewey's 189, with Strom Thurmond, running as the States' Rights candidate, receiving 39 Electoral votes. Truman won the election with less than 50% of the popular votes, with additional candidate, Henry Wallace, siphoning off over one million votes in the four man race.

December 15, 1948 - Alger Hiss, former State Department official, is indicted for perjury in connection to denials of passing state secrets to a communist spy ring. He would be convicted of the conspiracy on January 21, 1950 and receive a five year sentence.

1949

March 2, 1949 - Captain James Gallagher lands the B-50 Lucky Lady II in Texas after completing the first around-the-world non-stop airplane flight. It was refueled four times in flight.

April 4, 1949 - NATO, the North American Treaty Organization, is formed by the United States, Canada, and ten Western European nations (Belgium, Denmark, France, Iceland, Italy, Luxembourg, Netherlands, Norway, Portugal, United Kingdom). The treaty stated that any attack against one nation would be considered an attack against them all.

June 29, 1949 - United States withdraws its troops from Korea.

October 7, 1949 - Tokyo Rose, the femme fatale of Japanese war broadcasts, is sentenced to ten years in prison. She would be paroled in 1956 and pardoned in 1977.

October 14, 1949 - Eleven leaders of the United States Communist party are convicted of advocating a violent insurrection and overthrow of the U.S. government. The Supreme Court would uphold the convictions on June 4, 1951.

U.S. Timeline: The 1950's - Two Cars in Every Garage

1950
January 14, 1950 - The United States recalls all consular officials from China after the seizure of the American consul general in Peking.

January 17, 1950 - The Brinks robbery in Boston occurs when eleven masked bandits steal $2.8 million from an armored car outside their express office.

April 1, 1950 - For the first time, the 1950 census counts a population in the United States over 150 million people. The 14% increase since the last census now showed a count of 150,697,361. The most populous state in the United States was New York, now followed by California. The geographic center of the United States population had now moved west into Richland County, Illinois, 8 miles north-northwest of Olney.

June 25, 1950 - The Korean War begins its three year conflict when troops of North Korea, backed with Soviet weaponry, invade South Korea. This act leads to U.S. involvement when two days later, the United States Air Force and Navy are ordered by President Truman to the peninsula. On June 30, ground forces and air strikes are approved against North Korea.

June 27, 1950 - Thirty-five military advisors are sent to South Vietnam to give military and economic aid to the anti-Communist government.

November 26, 1950 - United Nations forces retreat south toward the 38th parallel when Chinese Communist forces open a counteroffensive in the Korean War. This action halted any thought of a quick resolution to the conflict. On December 8, 1950, shipments to Communist China are banned by the United States.

1951
February 28, 1951 - Preliminary report from the Senator Estes Kefauver investigation that had begun on May 11, 1950 into organized crime is issued, stating that gambling take was in excess of $20 billion per year.

March 29, 1951 - Julius and Ethel Rosenberg were found guilty of conspiracy of wartime espionage and sentenced to death. They were executed June 19, 1953. Morton Sobell was also convicted of the crime and sentenced to thirty years in prison.

September 1, 1951 - The United States, Australia, and New Zealand sign a mutual security pact, the ANZUS Treaty.

September 4, 1951 - The inauguration of trans-continental television occurs with the broadcast of President Truman's speech at the Japanese Peace Treaty Conference in San Francisco. The treaty would be signed on September 8 by the U.S., Japan, and forty-seven other nations.

December 12, 1951 - Richard Buckminster Fuller files patent for the Geodesic Dome. The dome building, under his design, would be utilized in many futuristic constructions, particularly by Fuller in world exhibitions, such as his famous United States Pavilion at the Montreal World's Fair of 1967.

1952
February 14, 1952 - The 1952 Winter Olympics open in Helsinki, Finland with thirty participating nations. During these games, the first triple jump in figure skating history is performed by Dick Button, who won one of the four gold medals gained by U.S. athletes.

April 8, 1952 - President Truman authorizes the seizure of United States steel mills in order to avert a strike, but his action is ruled illegal by the U.S. Supreme Court on June 2.

November 1, 1952 - At Eniwetok Atoll in the Pacific Ocean, the first hydrogen bomb, named Mike, is exploded.

November 4, 1952 - General Dwight D. Eisenhower, a newcomer to politics, but popular due to his role in winning World War II as European commander, gains an easy victory over Democratic challenger Adlai E. Stevenson. The Electoral College vote was 442 to 89.

November 29, 1952 - President-elect Dwight D. Eisenhower

travels to Korea to try and end the conflict.

1953
April 25, 1953 - The description of a double helix DNA molecule is published by British physicist Francis Crick and American scientist James D. Watson. They, along with New Zealand born scientist Maurice Wilkins, were awarded the Nobel Prize in Physiology or Medicine for their discovery in 1962.

July 27, 1953 - Fighting ceases in the Korean War. North Korea, South Korea, the United States, and the Republic of China sign an armistice agreement.

August 19, 1953 - The United States CIA assists in the overthrow of the government in Iran, and retains the Shah Mohammad Reza Pahlavi to the throne.

October 30, 1953 - The Cold War continues in earnest when President Dwight D. Eisenhower approves a top secret document stating that the U.S. nuclear arsenal must be expanded to combat the communist threat around the world.

December 30, 1953 - The first color televisions go on sale.

1954
February 23, 1953 - The first large scale vaccination of children against polio begins in Pittsburgh, Pennsylvania.

April 22, 1954 - Joseph McCarthy begins televised Senate hearings into alleged Communist influence in the United States Army. Later this year, on December 2, the U.S. Congress votes to condemn Senator McCarthy for his conduct during the Army investigation hearings.

May 17, 1954 - Racial segregation in public schools is declared unconstitutional by the United States Supreme Court in Brown vs. the Board of Education. The ruling of the court stated that racial segregation violated the 14th Amendment's clause that guaranteed equal protection. The Monroe School in Topeka, Kansas had segregated Linda Brown in its classes.

September 8, 1954 - In Bangkok, Thailand, the Southeast Asia

Treaty Organization is formed by the U.S., Great Britain, Australia, New Zealand, France, the Philippines, Pakistan, and Thailand, creating a mutual defense pact.

In 1954, Ray Kroc founds the idea for the McDonald's corporation, agreeing to franchise the idea of Dick and Mac McDonald, who had started the first McDonald's restaurant in 1940 and had eight restaurants by 1954. Kroc would incorporate the entity on March 2, 1955 and open his first franchise on April 15 in Des Plaines, Illinois. He would buy out the McDonald's brothers in 1961.

1955
February 12, 1955 - The United States government agrees to train South Vietnamese troops.

May 31, 1955 - The Supreme Court of the United States orders that all public schools be integrated with deliberate speed.

July 17-18, 1955 - The brainchild of Walt Disney, whose father had worked at previous world's fair and inspired his son, Disneyland, opens in Anaheim, California, with the backing of the new television network, ABC.

December 1, 1955 - Rosa Parks, an African American seamstress, refuses to give up her seat on the bus to a white man, prompting a boycott that would lead to the declaration that bus segregation laws were unconstitutional by a federal court.

December 5, 1955 - The two largest American labor unions, the American Federation of Labor and the Congress of Industrial Organizations, merge to form the AFL-CIO, boasting membership of fifteen million.

1956
March 12, 1956 - Congressmen from Southern states call for massive resistance, the Southern Manifesto, to the Supreme Court ruling on desegregation.

June 29, 1956 - Interstate highway system begins with the signing of the Federal-Aid Highway Act.

September 25, 1956 - The first transatlantic telephone cable begins operation.

October 8, 1956 - Dan Larsen pitches the first no-hitter, a perfect game, in post-season baseball history when his New York Yankees best the Brooklyn Dodgers in the 5th game of the 1956 World Series.

November 6, 1956 - A repeat challenge in the presidential election between Eisenhower and Stevenson gains a similar outcome, with easy victory for the incumbent president by a 457 to 73 margin in the Electoral College vote.

1957
January 20, 1957 - President Dwight D. Eisenhower is inaugurated for his second term in office.

March 13, 1957 - The Federal Bureau of Investigation arrests labor leader Jimmy Hoffa under a bribery charge.

April 29, 1957 - U.S. Congress approves the first civil rights bill since reconstruction with additional protection of voting rights.

September 4, 1957 - National Guard called to duty by Arkansas Governor Orval Faubus to bar nine black students from attending previously all-white Central High School in Little Rock, Arkansas. He withdrew the troops on September 21 and the students were allowed entrance to class two days later. A threat of violence caused President Eisenhower to dispatch federal troops to Little Rock on September 24 to enforce the edict.

December 6, 1957 - The first attempt by the United States to launch a satellite into space fails when it explodes on the launchpad.

Gordon Gould, an American physicist, invents the laser, It would take him until 1977 to win a protracted legal battle over patent rights, and he did not start receiving royalties on his work until 1988. Gould was elected to the National Inventors Hall of Fame in 1991.

1958

January 31, 1958 - Explorer I, the first U.S. space satellite, is launched by the Army at Cape Canaveral. It would discover the Van Allen radiation belt.

April 17, 1958 - The first major world's fair since the end of World War II opens in Brussels, Belgium and evokes a Cold War debate between the pavilions of the Soviet Union and the United States. Their competing visions of the world vie for the attention of the over 41 million visitors to the event, also noted for the Atomium atom molecular structure that stood as the fair's theme. The expo, sanctioned by the Bureau of International Exhibitions, closed on October 19, 1958.

July 8, 1958 - The Lituya Bay, Alaska earthquake registers 7.5 on the Richter scale, producing a landslide that caused a mega-tsunami with a 520 meter high wave. Only two people were killed in the incident, due to the desolate nature of the area involved. The wave dissipated when reaching the open sea.

December 10, 1958 - Jet airline passenger service is inaugurated in the United States by National Airlines with a flight between New York City and Miami, Florida.

1959

January 3, 1959 - Alaska is admitted to the United States as the 49th state to be followed on August 21 by Hawaii.

January 7, 1959 - The United States recognizes the new Cuban government under rebel leader Fidel Castro. Castro becomes the Premier of Cuba on February 16.

February 22, 1959 - The Daytona 500 stock car race is run for the first time with Lee Petty taking the first checkered flag.

April 9, 1959 - NASA selects the first seven military pilots to become the Mercury Seven, first astronauts of the United States. The Mercury Seven included John Glenn, Scott Carpenter, Gordon Cooper, Gus Griscom, Wally Scare, Alan Shepard, and Deke Slayton.

April 25, 1959 - The St. Lawrence Seaway is opened along the

Canada and United States borders, allowing increased ship traffic between the Atlantic Ocean and the Great Lakes.

September 26, 1959 - President Dwight D. Eisenhower hosts Soviet premier Nikita Khrushchev at his farm in Gettysburg, Pennsylvania during the first visit of any Soviet Union leader to the United States.

U.S. Timeline: The 1960's - Civil Rights and Turmoil

1960
February 1, 1960 - Four black college students from North Carolina Agricultural and Technical College in Greensboro, North Carolina stage a sit-in at a segregated Woolworth lunch counter, protesting their denial of service. This action caused a national campaign, waged by seventy-thousand students, both white and black, over the next eight months, in sit-ins across the nation for Civil Rights.

April 1, 1960 - Tiros I, the first weather satellite, is launched by the United States. Twelve days later, the navigation satellite, Transat 1-b is launched.

April 1, 1960 - The 1960 census includes a United States population of 179,323,175, an 18.5% increase since 1950. For the first time, two states, New York and California have over fifteen million people within their borders. The geographic center of the United States is located six and one half miles northwest of Centralia, Illinois.

May 1, 1960 - In the Soviet Union, a United States U-2 reconnaissance plane is shot done by Soviet forces, leading to the capture of U.S. pilot Gary Powers and the eventual cancellation of the Paris summit conference. On August 19, Powers is sentenced by the Soviet Union to ten years in prison for espionage. On February 10, 1962 , he would be exchanged for a captured Soviet spy in Berlin.

July 4, 1960 - The fifty star flag of the United States is debuted in Philadelphia, Pennsylvania, reflecting the admission of Hawaii into the union in 1959.

November 8, 1960 - The presidential race to succeed two term president Dwight D. Eisenhower is won by Senator John F. Kennedy, the Democratic candidate from Massachusetts, over incumbent Vice President Richard M. Nixon. Kennedy was a narrow victor in the popular vote, by slightly more than 120,000 votes, but won a more substantial victory in the Electoral College tally, 303 to 219. 62.8% of the voting age population took part in the contest. The 1960 campaign for president had seen the first televised debate on September 26.

1961
January 3, 1961 - Disputes over the nationalization of United States businesses in Cuba cause the U.S. Government to sever diplomatic and consular relations with the Cuban government.

February 15, 1961 - The entire United States figure skating team is killed in a plane crash near Brussels, Belgium on their journey to the World Championships. Seventy-three people are killed.

April 17, 1961 - The Bay of Pigs invasion of Cuba is repulsed by Cuban forces in an attempt by Cuban exiles under the direction of the United States government to overthrow the regime of Fidel Castro.

May 5, 1961 - The first U.S. manned sub-orbital space flight is completed with Commander Alan B. Shepard Jr. inside a Mercury capsule launched 116.5 miles above the earth from Cape Canaveral, Florida. Twenty days later, President Kennedy announces his intention to place a man on the moon by the end of the decade.

August 13, 1961 - The construction of the Berlin Wall begins by the Soviet bloc, segregating the German city, previously held in four sectors by Allied forces, including the United States. The wall would last for twenty-eight years.

December 28, 1961 - The National Park Service extends its lands into the U.S. Virgin Islands when President John F. Kennedy proclaims the Buck Island Reef as a National Monument. The reef includes an underwater nature trail and one of the best marine gardens in the Caribbean Sea.

1962
February 7, 1962 - The first sign of a looming Vietnam conflict emerges when President Kennedy admits that the military advisors already in Vietnam would engage the enemy if fired upon.

February 20, 1962 - Lt. Colonel John Glenn becomes the first U.S. astronaut in orbit in the Friendship 7 Mercury capsule. He would circle the earth three times before returning to earth, remaining aloft for four hours and fifty-five minutes. This flight equalized the space race with the Soviet Union, whose Vostok I flight on April 12, 1961 with Yuri Gagarin had become the first manned spaceflight into orbit one year earlier.

April 21, 1962 - The Seattle Century 21 Exposition, the first world's fair held in the United States since World War II, opens under the theme of space exploration. Over 9.6 million visitors would attend the exposition over 184 days in central Seattle, whose monorail still travels inside the city.

October 1, 1962 - Three thousand troops quell riots, allowing James Meredith to enter the University of Mississippi as the first black student under guard by Federal marshals.

October 14, 1962 - The Cuban Missile Crises begins. In response to the Soviet Union building offensive missiles in Cuba, President John F. Kennedy orders a naval and air blockade of military equipment to the island. An agreement is eventually reached with Soviet Premier Khrushchev on the removal of the missiles, ending the potential conflict after thirty-eight days, in what many think was the closest the Cold War came to breaking into armed conflict.

1963
March 21, 1963 - The last twenty-seven prisoners of Alcatraz, the island prison in San Francisco Bay, are ordered removed by Attorney General Robert F. Kennedy, and the federal penitentiary is closed.

June 11, 1963 - A patent for the first manned space capsule, the Mercury, is issued to Maxime A. Faget, Andre J. Meyer, Jr., Robert G. Chilton, William S. Blanchard, Jr., Alan B. Kehlet, Jerome B. Hammack, and Caldwell C. Johnson, Jr.

June 17, 1963 - The Supreme Court of the United States ruled in the case of Abington School District vs. Schempp that laws requiring the recitation of the Lord's Prayer or Bible verses in public schools is unconstitutional. The vote was 8 to 1.

July 25, 1963 - The United States, Soviet Union, and Great

Britain agree to a limited nuclear test-ban treaty, barring all nuclear testing above ground.

August 28, 1963 - The Civil Rights march on Washington, D.C. for Jobs and Freedom culminates with Dr. Martin Luther King's famous "I Have a Dream" speech from the steps of the Lincoln Memorial. Over 200,000 people participated in the march for equal rights.

August 29, 1963 - A peaceful settlement to the land dispute between Mexico and the United States is enacted with the signing of the Chamizal Treaty, establishing the boundary in the El Paso Juarez Valley. The dispute, which had been ongoing for ninety-nine years, is now commemorated by the Chamizal National Memorial in El Paso, Texas.

November 22, 1963 - In Dallas, Texas, during a motorcade through downtown, President John F. Kennedy is mortally wounded by assassin Lee Harvey Oswald. Vice President Lyndon B. Johnson is sworn into office later that day. Two days later, Oswald was himself killed on live national television by Jack Ruby while being transported in police custody.

1964
January 9, 1964 - The Panama Canal incident occurs when Panamanian mobs engage United States troops, leading to the death of twenty-one Panama citizens and four U.S. troops.

January 13, 1964 - Beatlemania hits the shores of the United States with the release of I Want to Hold Your Hand, which becomes the Liverpool group's first North American hit. One week later, their first U.S. album Meet the Beatles is released.

February 25, 1964 - 1960 Olympic champion Cassius Clay (Muhammad Ali) wins the World Heavyweight Championship in Boxing from current champ Sonny Liston.

April 22, 1964 - The New York World's War opens in Queens, New York on the site of the 1939 event. One of the largest world's fairs in United States history, it was not a sanctioned Bureau of International Exhibitions event, due to conflict over the dates of the Seattle fair of 1962. This world's fair would last for two seasons, and included exhibits from eighty nations. Over 50 million visitors would attend. Its theme structure, the Unisphere, is still present, now seen each August outside the U.S. Tennis Open.

June 29, 1964 - An omnibus legislation in the U.S. Congress on Civil Rights is passed. It banned discrimination in jobs, voting and accommodations.

August 7, 1964 - The Tonkin Resolution is passed by the United States Congress, authorizing broad powers to the president to take action in Vietnam after North Vietnamese boats had attacked two United States destroyers five days earlier.

November 3, 1964 - President Lyndon B. Johnson wins his first presidential election with a victory over Barry M. Goldwater from Arizona. Johnson extended the Democratic victory by former running mate John F. Kennedy with a 486 to 52 thrashing of the Republican candidate in the Electoral College and over 15 million surplus in the popular vote.

1965
February 7, 1965 - President Lyndon B. Johnson orders the continuous bombing of North Vietnam below the 20th parallel.

March 25, 1965 - Martin Luther King speaks at a civil rights rally on the courthouse steps of the Alabama State Capitol, ending the Selma to Montgomery, Alabama march for voting rights.

August 6, 1965 - The Voting Rights Act of 1965 is signed into law by President Lyndon B. Johnson. Two significant portions of the act; the outlawing of the requirement of potential voters to take a literacy test in order to qualify and the provision of federal registration of voters in areas with less than 50% of all voters registered.

August 11, 1965 - The Watts race riots in Los Angeles begin a five day siege, culminating in the death of thirty-four people and property destruction in excess of $200 million.

October 15, 1965 - The first public burning of a draft card occurs in protest to the Vietnam War. It is coordinated by the anti-war group of students, National Coordinating Committee to End the War in Vietnam.

Kevlar is developed by Dupont scientist Stephanie Louise Kwolek. She would patent the compound, used extensively in bullet proof vests, in 1966.

1966
June 29, 1966 - United States warplanes begin their bombing raids of Hanoi and Haiphong, North Vietnam. By December of this year, the United States had 385,300 troops stationed in South Vietnam with sixty thousand additional troops offshore and thirty-three thousand in Thailand.

July 1, 1966 - Medicare, the government medical program for citizens over the age of 65, begins.

September 9, 1966 - President Lyndon Johnson signed legislation creating the San Juan Island National Historical Park. The site, in Washington State, includes the location of British and United States army camps in the 1860s when both nations claimed ownership of the island.

October 15, 1966 - The National Historic Preservation Act is made law. It expanded the National Register of Historic Places to include historic sites of regional, state, and local significance.

November 8, 1966 - The first black United States Senator in eighty-five years, Edward Brooke, is elected to Congress. Brooke was the Republican candidate from Massachusetts and former Attorney General of that state.

1967
January 27, 1967 - The Outer Space Treaty is signed into force by the United States, Great Britain, and the Soviet Union, to take effect on October 10, 1967.

June 23, 1967 - A three day summit between President Lyndon B. Johnson and Soviet Premier Alexei Kosygin, held at Glassboro State College in New Jersey, culminates in a mutual declaration that no crises between them would lead to war.

July 1967 - Black riots plague U.S. cities. In Newark, New Jersey, twenty-six are killed, fifteen hundred injured and one thousand arrested from July 12 to 17. One week later, July 23 to 30, forty are killed, two thousand injured, and five thousand left homeless after rioting in Detroit, known as the 12th Street Riots, decimate a black ghetto. The riots are eventually stopped by over 12,500 Federal troopers and National Guardsmen.

October 2, 1967 - Thurgood Marshall is sworn into office as the first black Supreme Court Justice.

1968
January 23, 1968 - The U.S.S. Pueblo incident occurs in the Sea of Japan when North Korea seizes the ship and its crew, accusing it of violating its territorial waters for the purpose of spying. They would release the prisoners on December 22, but North Korea still holds possession of the U.S.S. Pueblo to this day.

February 13, 1968 - Ford's Theatre, the site of the assassination of President Abraham Lincoln in 1865 in Washington, D.C., reopens to the public. It had been restored to its original appearance and use as a theatre, now comprising the Ford's Theatre National Historic Site.

March 31, 1968 - President Johnson announces a slowing to the bombing of North Vietnam, and that he would not seek reelection as president. Peace talks would begin May 10 in Paris; all bombing of North Korea halted October 31.

April 4, 1968 - Civil Rights leader Martin Luther King is assassinated in Memphis, Tennessee while standing on a motel balcony by James Earl Ray.

June 5, 1968 - Presidential candidate, the Democratic Senator from New York, Robert F. Kennedy, is shot at a campaign victory celebration in Los Angeles by Sirhan Sirhan, a Jordanian, after primary victories, and dies one day later.

November 5, 1968 - Richard M. Nixon recaptures the White House from the Democratic party with his victory of Hubert H. Humphrey and 3rd Party candidate George Wallace. Nixon captures 301 Electoral College Votes to 191 for Humphrey and 46 for Wallace.

1969
January 12, 1969 - The New York Jets win Super Bowl III over the Baltimore Colts after a bold prediction by quarterback Joe Namath. This is the first victory in the National Football League for a former American Football League team.

January 25, 1969 - Four-party Vietnam war peace talks begin. In April, U.S. troops in the war reached its zenith at 543,400 and would begin their withdrawal on July 8.

July 20, 1969 - The Apollo program completes its mission. Neil Armstrong, United States astronaut, becomes the first man to set foot on the moon four days after launch from Cape Canaveral. His Apollo 11 colleague, Edwin E. Aldrin, Jr. accompanies him.

July 25, 1969 - President Richard M. Nixon announces his new Vietnam policy, declaring the Nixon Doctrine that expected Asian allies to care for their own military defense. This policy, and all Vietnam war policies, would be heavily protested throughout the remainder of the year. On November 15, 1969, more than two hundred and fifty thousand anti-Vietnam war demonstrators marched on Washington, D.C. to peacefully protest the war.

November 20, 1969 - Alcatraz Island, the former prison in San Francisco Bay, is occupied by fourteen American Indians in a long standoff over the issues of Indian causes.

November 21, 1969 - The Internet, called Arpanet during its initial development, is invented by the Advanced Research Projects Agency at the U.S. Department of Defense. The first operational packet switching network in the world was deployed connecting the IMP at UCLA and the Stanford Research Institute. By December 5, it included the entire four node system, with the UCSB and the University of Utah.

1970
February 18, 1970 - Five members of the Chicago 7 are convicted of crossing state lines to incite riots during the 1968 Democratic Presidential Convention in Chicago.

April 1, 1970 - For the first time, the 1970 census counted over 200 million people living in the United States. The 13.4% increase since the last census indicated that a 203,302,031 population now called the U.S.A. home. It had taken only fifty years to go from the first 100 million census in 1920 to the second. Once again, the geographic center of the United States population was in Illinois, five miles east southeast of Mascoutah.

April 22, 1970 - The first Earth Day celebration is held with millions of Americans participating in anti-pollution demonstrations. These demonstrations included school children walking to school instead of riding the bus.

May 4, 1970 - Four students from Kent State University in Ohio were killed and nine wounded by National Guardsmen during a protest against the Vietnam War spread into Cambodia.

August 12, 1970 - The United States Postal Service is made independent in a postal reform measure for the first time in almost two centuries.

1971
January 2, 1971 - A ban on the television advertisement of cigarettes goes into affect in the United States.

February 8, 1971 - A forty-four day raid into Laos by South Vietnamese soldiers is begun with the aid of United States air and artillery.

March 10, 1971 - The Senate approves a Constitutional Amendment, the 26th, that would lower the voting age from 21 to 18. House approval came on March 23. It was ratified by the states by June 30 and received certification by President Richard M. Nixon on July 5.

June 30, 1971 - The United States Supreme Court upholds the right of the New York Times and the Washington Post to publish classified Pentagon papers about the Vietnam War, under the articles of the First Amendment to the Constitution. The New York Times had begun the publication of the Pentagon papers on June 13.

September 17, 1971 - The advent of the microprocessor age at Texas Instruments includes the introduction of the 4-bit TMS 1000 with a calculator on the chip; on November 15, 1971, Intel released the 4-bit 4004 microprocessor developed by Federico Faggin. It is unknown whose chip predated the other in the laboratory environment.

October 1, 1971 - Walt Disney World opens in Orlando, Florida, expanding the Disney empire to the east coast of the United States.

1972
February 21, 1972 - The journey for peace trip of the U.S. President to Peking, China begins. The eight day journey by Richard M. Nixon and meetings with Mao Zedong, unprecedented at the time, began the process for normalization of relations with China.

March 30, 1972 - The largest attacks by North Vietnam troops across the demilitarized zone in four years prompts bombing raids to begin again by United States forces against Hanoi and Haiphong on April 15, ending a four year cessation of those raids.

May 22, 1972 - President Richard M. Nixon makes the first trip of the U.S. President to Moscow. The week of summit discussions would lead to a strategic arms pact, SALT I that would be signed by Nixon and Premier Leonid Brezhnev on May 26. On July 8, the White House would announce the sale of American wheat to the Soviet Union.

June 17, 1972 - The Watergate crisis begins when four men are arrested for breaking into the Democratic National Committee headquarters in the Watergate office building in Washington, D.C. on the same day that Okinawa is returned from U.S. control back to Japan.

November 7, 1972 - In one of the most lopsided races in American Presidential election history, incumbent President Richard M. Nixon beat his Democratic challenger George S. McGovern, winning 520 Electoral College votes to McGovern's 17, and taking over 60% of the popular vote. This election, however, would be the beginning of the end for the presidency of Richard M. Nixon, once the Watergate affair brought question into the tactics within the election process.

1973
January 22, 1973 - The United States Supreme Court rules in Roe vs. Wade that a woman can not be prevented by a state in having an abortion during the first six months of pregnancy.

January 27, 1973 - Four part Vietnam peace pacts, the Paris Peace Accords, were signed in Paris, France. The announcement of the military draft ending also occurred on that date. The last U.S. military troops would leave the war zone on March 29.

January 30, 1973 - Two defendants in the Watergate break-in trial are convicted. The remaining five defendants had pleaded guilty to the crime two weeks earlier. On April 30, the Watergate affair widens when four members of the Nixon administration; aides H.R. Haldeman, John D. Ehrlichman, John W. Dean, and Attorney General Richard Kleindienst resign under suspicion of obstructing justice. During Senate hearings on June 25, Dean would admit that the administration had conspired to cover up facts about the case, leading to the refusal of the President to release tapes concerning Watergate.

June 9, 1973 - In one of the most awesome displays of dominance in sports history, Secretariat, wins the Belmont Stakes by 31 lengths, winning the Triple Crown of United States Thoroughbred Racing for the first time since 1948.

October 10, 1973 - Vice President Spiro T. Agnew resigns amid charges of tax evasion and is replaced by the appointment of Gerald R. Ford on October 12.

October 19, 1973 - The Arab Oil Embargo: Oil imports from Arab oil-producing nations are banned to the United States after the start of the Arab-Israeli war, creating the 1973 energy crisis. They would not resume until March 18, 1974.

1974
March 7, 1974 - Legislation is signed by President Nixon creating the Big South Fork National River and Recreation Area along the Cumberland River in Kentucky and Tennessee.

May 4, 1974 - Expo '74, the Bureau of International Exhibitions sanctioned special exposition was held for six months in the Washington State city of Spokane, one of the smaller cities to host a BIE world expo in their history. Held on the theme "Celebrating Tomorrow's Fresh, Clean Environment," the event capitalized on the Earth Day sentiments of the time, and drew over 5 million visitors to eastern Washington State.

May 7, 1974 - Impeachment hearings are begun by the House Judiciary Committee against President Richard M. Nixon in the Watergate affair. On July 24, the United States Supreme Court rules that President Nixon must turn over the sixty-four tapes of White House conversations concerning the Watergate break-in.

July 27, 1974 - The first of three articles of impeachment against President Richard M. Nixon is recommended in a 27-11 vote of the House Judiciary Committee, charging that Nixon had been part of a criminal conspiracy to obstruct justice in the Watergate affair.

August 9, 1974 - President Richard M. Nixon resigns the office of the presidency, avoiding the impeachment process and admitting his role in the Watergate affair. He was replaced by Vice President Gerald R. Ford, who, on September 8, 1974, pardoned Nixon for his role. Nixon was the first president to ever resign from office.

1975
January 1, 1975 - The Watergate cover up trials of Mitchell, Haldeman, and Ehrlichman are completed; all are found guilty of the charges.

January 6, 1975 - The television show Wheel of Fortune premiers.

February 4, 1975 - Heiress Patty Hearst is kidnaped in San Francisco. She would be recovered by FBI agents on September 8 and subsequently indicted for bank robbery. Hearst would be convicted of the crime two years later.

March 30, 1975 - At the railroad depot in Plains, Georgia, his home town, former Democratic Georgia governor Jimmy Carter opens his campaign headquarters for the 1976 presidential race.

April 29-30, 1975 - Communist forces complete their takeover of South Vietnam, forcing the evacuation from Saigon of civilians from the United States and the unconditional surrender of South Vietnam.

1976
July 4, 1976 - The Bicentennial of the United States is celebrated throughout the nation. The 200th anniversary included Operation Sail in New York City, as well as a Bicentennial Wagon Train that traversed the nation during the year.

July 20, 1976 - The Viking 1 space probe successfully lands on Mars. It would be followed by a second unmanned Viking II on the Utopia Plains on September 3. The first color photos of the surface of Mars are taken on these flights.

July 21-24, 1976 - Twenty-nine people attending an American Legion convention in Philadelphia are killed by a mysterious ailment, one year later discovered as a bacterium.

November 2, 1976 - Challenger Jimmy Carter, a relatively unknown former Democratic governor from Georgia, bests Gerald Ford in a closely contested election. Carter received a slight majority of the popular vote, as well as an Electoral College victory of 297 to 240.

November 26, 1976 - Microsoft becomes a registered trademark, one year after its name for microcomputer software is first mentioned by Bill Gates to Paul Allen in a letter.

1977

January 21, 1977 - The majority of Vietnam War draft evaders, ten thousand in number, are pardoned by President Jimmy Carter.

May 25, 1977 - The movie Star Wars opens and becomes the highest grossing film at the time.

August 4, 1977 - The cabinet level Energy Department is created by Jimmy Carter.

July 13, 1977 - The New York City blackout results in massive looting and disorderly conduct during its twenty-five hour duration.

September 21, 1977 - Fifteen nations, including the United States and the Soviet Union, sign a nuclear-proliferation pact, slowing the spread of nuclear weapons around the world.

1978

March 3, 1978 - In one of the first articles on the subject of human cloning, the New York Post prints an article on the book The Cloning of Man which supposes the cloning of a human being.

April 18, 1978 - The United States Senate votes to return the Panama Canal back to Panama on December 31, 1999. A treaty for the return had been signed on September 7 of the previous year, pending approval by the U.S. Congress.

August 17, 1978 - The first balloon, Double Eagle II, to cross the Atlantic Ocean comes to rest in Miserey, France, after one hundred and thirty-seven hours of flight from Presque Isle, Maine.

September 17, 1978 - The Camp David Peace Agreement between Israel and Egypt is formulated in twelve days of secret negotiations at the Camp David retreat of the President. President Jimmy Carter witnessed the signing of the agreement between Israeli Prime Minister Menachem Begin and Egyptian President Anwar Sadat at the White House.

October 16, 1978 - Pope John Paul II, Karol Wojtyla of Poland, is elected Pope at Vatican City.

1979
March 28, 1979 - An accident at the Three Mile Island nuclear power plant in Middletown, Pennsylvania occurs when a partial core meltdown is recorded. A tense situation ensued for five days until the reactor was deemed under control. It is the largest accident in U.S. nuclear power history and considered the worst in the world until the Soviet Chernobyl accident seven years later.

September 1, 1979 - The American Pioneer Eleven passes the planet Saturn, becoming the first spacecraft to visit the ringed planet, albeit at a distance of 21,000 kilometers.

October 6, 1979 - The Federal Reserve system changes its monetary policy goals from interest rate based to a money supply target orientation.

November 1, 1979 - The Chrysler Bailout is approved by the federal government. A $1.5 billion loan-guarantee plan is floated to assist the third largest car maker in the United States.

November 4, 1979 - The Iran Hostage Crisis begins when sixty-three Americans are among ninety hostages taken at the American embassy in Tehran by three thousand militant student followers of Ayatollah Khomeini, who demand that the former shah return to Iran to stand trial.

1980

January 4, 1980 - President Jimmy Carter announces the embargo on sale of grain and high technology to the Soviet Union due to the Soviet invasion of Afghanistan.

February 13, 1980 - The opening ceremonies of the 1980 Winter Olympics Games are held in Lake Placid, New York. One of the most thrilling moments include the Miracle on Ice when a team of U.S. amateur ice hockey players defeated the vaunted Soviet Union professional all-star team in the semi-final game, then won the gold medal over Finland. U.S. speed skater Eric Heiden also concluded one of the most amazing feats in sports history when he won all five speed skating medals from the sprint at 500 meters to the marathon 10,000 meter event.

April 1, 1980 - The 1980 census shows a population in the United States of 226,542,203, an 11.4% increase since 1970. For the first time, one state had over 20 million people living within its borders, the state of California with 23.7 million. Due to a trend of western migration, Missouri now contained the geographic population center of the United States, one quarter mile west of De Soto in Jefferson County.

April 12, 1980 - The United States Olympic Committee, responding to the request of President Jimmy Carter on March 21, votes to withdraw its athletes from participation in the Moscow Summer Olympic Games due to the continued involvement of the Soviet Union in Afghanistan.

April 24-25, 1980 - The attempt to rescue the American hostages held captive in the U.S. Embassy in Iran fails with eight Americans killed and five wounded in Operation Eagle Claw when a mid-air collision occurs.

May 18, 1980 - The Mt. St. Helens volcano, in Washington State, erupts, killing fifty-seven people and economic devastation to the area with losses near $3 billion. The blast was estimated to have the power five hundred times greater than the Hiroshima atomic bomb.

October 10, 1980 - President Carter signs legislation establishing Boston African American National Historic Site, which includes the oldest black church in America and other historic sites of the Black Heritage Trail in Boston, Massachusetts.

November 4, 1980 - Ronald Reagan, the former Republican governor of California, beats President Jimmy Carter and independent candidate John B. Anderson, also a Republican, in a landslide victory, ousting the incumbent from office. The victory in the Electoral College, 489 to 49, as well as an 8 million vote margin in the popular vote over Carter, ensured a mandate for the new president.

1981
January 20, 1981 - The inauguration of Ronald Reagan as the 40th president of the United States occurs in Washington, D.C. It was followed by the release of the fifty-two Americans still held hostage in Tehran. The Iranian hostage crisis, which lasted four hundred and forty-four days, was negotiated for the return of $8 billion in frozen Iranian assets.

March 30, 1981 - President Ronald Reagan withstands an assassination attempt, shot in the chest while walking to his limousine in Washington, D.C.

April 12, 1981 - The first launch of the Space Shuttle from Cape Canaveral and the Kennedy Space Center occurs as Columbia begins its STS-1 mission. The Space Shuttle is the first reusable spacecraft to be flown into orbit, and it returned to earth for a traditional touch down landing two days later.

July 29, 1981 - Tax cut legislation proposed by President Ronald Reagan, the largest in history, is passed by both houses of the U.S. Congress. It would reduce taxes by $750 billion over the next five years.

August 12, 1981 - IBM introduces the IBM-PC personal computer, the IBM 5150. It was designed by twelve engineers and designers under Don Estridge of the IBM Entry Systems Division. It sold for $1,565 in 1981.

September 21, 1981 - Sandra Day O'Connor is approved

unanimously, 99-0, by the United States Senate to become the first female Supreme Court associate justice in history.

1982
January 8, 1982 - ATT settles its lawsuit with the U.S. Justice Department. The agreement forced the independence of the twenty-two regional Bell System companies in return for expansion into the prohibited areas of data processing and equipment sales.

March 2, 1982 - The Senate passes a bill that virtually eliminated the practice of busing to achieve racial integration.

May 1, 1982 - The Knoxville World's Fair opens on the topic of energy by President Reagan. A special category exposition sanctioned by the Bureau of International Exhibitions, the Knoxville event would draw over eleven million people to the Tennessee valley over the next six months.

November 5, 1982 - The highest unemployment rate since 1940 is recorded at 10.4%. By the end of November, over eleven million people would be unemployed.

November 13, 1982 - The Vietnam Veterans Memorial is dedicated in Washington, D.C., holding the names of the more than 58,000 killed or missing in action during the conflict.

1983
March 23, 1983 - The initial proposal to develop technology to intercept incoming missiles, the Strategic Defense Initiative Program, or Star Wars, is made by President Ronald Reagan.

April 20, 1983 - President Reagan signs legislation meant to rescue the Social Security System from bankruptcy.

June 18, 1983 - Astronaut Sally Ride becomes the first American woman to travel into space.

October 23, 1983 - A terrorist truck bomb kills two hundred and forty-one United States peacekeeping troops in Lebanon at Beirut International Airport. A second bomb destroyed a French barracks two miles away, killing forty there.

October 25, 1983 - The United States invasion of Grenada occurs at the request of the Organization of Eastern Caribbean States to depose the Marxist regime.

1984

February 7, 1984 - Navy Captain Bruce McCandless and Army Lt. Colonel Robert Stewart become the first astronauts to fly free of a spacecraft in orbit during a space shuttle flight that began four days earlier.

May 12, 1984 - The Louisiana World Exposition of 1984 opens along the Mississippi River waterfront in New Orleans. The event, the last world's fair held in the United States, was plagued with financial trouble, and drew significantly fewer visitors than predicted over the next six months, 7.3 million, although it was regarded as the catalyst in the recovery of the waterfront and warehouse district to public use.

July 12, 1984 - Democratic candidate for President, Walter Mondale, selects Geraldine Ferraro as his Vice Presidential running mate, the first woman chosen for that position.

July 28, 1984 - The opening ceremony of the Los Angeles Olympic Games is held. The games run by Peter Ueberroth, prove a financial and U.S. success, despite a retaliatory boycott by most allies of the Soviet Union due to the U.S. boycott of the 1980 Moscow games.

November 6, 1984 - President Ronald Reagan wins reelection over Democratic challenger Walter F. Mondale, increasing his Electoral College victory since the 1980 election to a margin of 525 to 13.

1985

July 13, 1985 - A famine relief concert organized by British artist Bob Geldof and held simultaneously in London and Philadelphia is seen in one hundred and fifty-two countries. The seventeen hour concert raised $70 million for relief efforts in Ethiopia and other African nations.

September 11, 1985 - Pete Rose breaks Ty Cobb's record for

most career hits in Major League Baseball history. He would be banned from baseball in 1989 for gambling, thus making him ineligible for election into the Baseball Hall of Fame in Cooperstown, New York.

November 19, 1985 - The first meeting in six years between the leaders of the Soviet Union and the United States occurs when Mikhail Gorbachev and Ronald Reagan engage in a five hour summit conference in Geneva, Switzerland.

November 20, 1985 - The first version of the Windows operating system for computers is released.

December 11, 1985 - General Electric Corporation agrees to buy RCA Corporation for $6.28 billion in the largest corporate merger ever outside the oil industry.

1986
January 20, 1986 - Martin Luther King Day is officially observed for the first time as a federal holiday in the United States.

January 28, 1986 - The Challenger Space Shuttle explodes after lift off at Cape Canaveral, Florida, killing seven people, including Christa McAuliffe, a New Hampshire school teacher.

May 25, 1986 - Five million people make a human chain across the United States in the Hands Across America campaign to fight hunger and homelessness.

September 18, 1986 - A tentative agreement on a world-wide ban on medium-range missiles is reached between the Soviet Union and the United States. This agreement would not be expanded to include long-range missiles when President Reagan refused capitulation to the demand from Mikhail Gorbachev to limit development of the Star Wars missile defense shield.

November 3, 1986 - The first reporting of the Iran-Contra affair, diverting money from arm sales to Iran to fund Nicaraguan contra rebels, begins the largest crisis in the Reagan tenure.

1987
August 12, 1987 - Near the end of hearings into the Iran-contra

affair, President Reagan admits to a policy that went astray, but denied knowledge of the diversion of funds to the contras.

October 19, 1987 - The stock market crash known as Black Monday occurs on the New York Stock Exchange, recording a record 22.6% drop in one day. Stock markets around the world would mirror the crash with drops of their own.

October 23, 1987 - The President's nominee to the Supreme Court, Robert Bork, is rejected by the U.S. Senate, 58-42, in the largest margin of rejection for the role in history.

December 8, 1987 - The United States and the Soviet Union sign an agreement, the Intermediate Range Nuclear Forces Treaty, to dismantle all 1,752 U.S. and 859 Soviet missiles in the 300-3,400 mile range.

December 31, 1987 - El Malpais National Monument in New Mexico is established by legislation. It preserved a natural volcanic area, a seventeen mile lava tube system, and remains from the Pueblo Indian culture.

1988
February 3, 1988 - The United States House of Representatives rejects the request of President Reagan for $36.25 million to fund the Nicaraguan Contras.

April 12, 1988 - The first patent for a genetically engineered animal is issued to Harvard University researchers Philip Leder and Timothy Stewart.

May 4, 1988 - The deadline for amnesty application by illegal aliens is met by 1.4 million applications. It is estimated that 71% of those who applied had entered the United States from Mexico.

October 31, 1988 - Poverty Point National Monument in Louisiana is established by President Ronald Reagan in order to preserve some of the most extensive earthworks from prehistoric times in North America.

November 8, 1988 - Vice President under Ronald Reagan, George Herbert Walker Bush, claims victory in the presidential election over Democratic challenger Michael S. Dukakis, Governor of Massachusetts. The Electoral College vote tallied 426 for Bush and 111 for Dukakis.

1989
January 6, 1989 - Economic reports on the previous year from the Labor Department indicate a growth rate of 3.8%, the largest in four years and an unemployment rate of 5.3%, a low of fourteen years.

March 24, 1989 - The Exxon Valdez crashes into Bligh Reef in Alaska's Prince William Sound, causing the largest oil spill in American history, eleven million gallons, which extended forty-five miles.

August 9, 1989 - The Savings and Loan Bailout is approved by Congress and signed into law by President George Herbert Walker Bush. The total cost of the bill would approach $400 billion over thirty years to close and merge insolvent Savings and Loans.

August 10, 1989 - Army General Colin Powell is elevated to the position of Chairman of the Joint Chiefs of Staff, becoming the first African American to be nominated to that post.

November 9, 1989 - The Berlin Wall, after thirty-eight years of restricting traffic between the East and West German sides of the city, begins to crumble when German citizens are allowed to travel freely between East and West Germany for the first time. One day later, the influx of crowds around and onto the wall begin to dismantle it, thus ending its existence.

U.S. Timeline: The 1990's -Prosperity as the World Turns

1990
February 7, 1990 - The Central Committee of the Soviet Communist Party gives up its monopoly of power, continuing the trend, since the beginning of the Berlin Wall coming down, that the Cold War was about to end. The ending of the Cold War was completed, in many ways, by the strong policies of U.S. President Ronald Reagan toward the Soviet block. Six days later, a plan to reunite Germany was announced.

March 18, 1990 - The largest art theft in U.S. history occurs in Boston, Massachusetts, when two thieves posing as policemen abscond twelve paintings worth an estimated $100-200 million from the Isabella Stewart Gardner Museum.

April 1, 1990 - The 1990 census is conducted, counting 248,718,301, for an increase of 9.8% over the 1980 census. This is the smallest increase in the population rate since 1940. The geographic center of the United States population is now ten miles southeast of Steelville, Missouri.

April 24, 1990 - The Hubble Telescope is placed into orbit by the United States Space Shuttle Discovery. One month later, the telescope becomes operational.

June 1, 1990 - U.S. President George H.W. Bush and his Soviet counterpart Mikhail Gorbachev sign a treaty to eliminate chemical weapon production and begin the destruction of each nation's current inventory.

August 2, 1990 - Iraq invades its neighbor, Kuwait, setting into motion the beginning of U.S. involvement in the Gulf War. Four days later, the United Nations begins a global trade embargo against Iraq. On November 29, the United Nations passes a resolution, #678, stating that Iraq must withdraw its forces from Kuwait by January 15, 1991 or face military intervention.

August 6, 1990 - Tumacacori National Monument is enlarged and re-titled a Historical Park by legislation signed into law by President George H.W. Bush. The site, including the historic Spanish mission church of San Jose de Tumacacori, was founded by Padre Eusebio Kino in 1691.

1991
January 12, 1991 - U.S. Congress passes a resolution authorizing the use of force to liberate Kuwait. Operation Desert Storm begins four days later with air strikes against Iraq. Iraq responds by sending eight Scud missiles into Israel.

February 27, 1991 - The Gulf War ends one day after Iraq withdraws its forces from Kuwait and sets the oil fields on fire. A cease fire is declared and Iraq accepts the condition of disarmament after one hundred hours of ground fighting. On April 3, the United Nations Security Council passes Resolution 687, calling for the destruction and removal of the entire Iraqi chemical and biological weapons stockpile, plus ballistic missiles with a range greater than 150 kilometers. Iraq also agrees to withdraw its support of international terrorism.

October 3, 1991 - The governor of Arkansas, William Jefferson Clinton, announces his intention to seek the 1992 Democratic nomination for the Presidency of the United States.

July 29, 1991 - Bank of Credit and Commerce International is indicted in New York for the largest bank fraud in history.

November 27, 1991 - The United Nations Security Council unanimously votes to adopt Resolution 721, which would lead the way to establishing peacekeeping forces in Yugoslavia. Three months later, another resolution would approve a peacekeeping force be sent.

1992
January 26, 1992 - The renewed nation of Russia, part of the Soviet Union dissolved on December 26, 1991, and their leader Boris Yeltsin announce that they will stop targeting the cities of the United States with nuclear weapons.

February 24, 1992 - The Salt River Bay National Historical Park and Ecological Preserve is established through legislation signed by President George H.W. Bush. The park in St. Croix, U.S. Virgin Islands is the only location under the jurisdiction of the United States where the men of Christopher Columbus are known to have been.

May 7, 1992 - The 27th Amendment to the Constitution is passed two hundred and two years after its initial proposal. It bars the United States Congress from giving itself a midterm or retroactive pay raise. This amendment had been originally proposed by James Madison in 1789, as part of twelve amendments, of which ten would become the original Bill of Rights on December 15, 1791.

August 21, 1992 - The Siege of Ruby Ridge is begun by United States Marshals, lasting ten days. The incident would end with the acquittal of all but one minor charge against the Weaver family and lead to admonishment of the handling of the incident by Federal authorities.

November 3, 1992 - In a three way race for the presidency of the United States, Democratic candidate Bill Clinton defeats incumbent President George H.W. Bush and businessman H. Ross Perot of the Reform Party. Many trace the loss of President Bush to his reneging a pledge for "no new taxes." Clinton received only 43% of the popular vote, but 370 Electoral votes to Bush with 37.4% and 168 Electoral College votes. Perot garnered 18.9% of the popular vote, but no Electoral College delegates.

1993
February 26, 1993 - The World Trade Center is bombed by Islamic terrorists when a van parked below the North Tower of the structure explodes. Six people are killed and over one thousand are injured.

February 28, 1993 - The fifty-one day Waco standoff begins when the Bureau of Alcohol, Tobacco, and Firearms attempt to arrest the Branch Davidian leader David Koresh on federal arms violations. Four agents and five members of the cult are killed in the raid. The siege would end on April 19 when a fire, started by the Davidians, killed seventy-five members of the group, including the leader.

June 27, 1993 - President Bill Clinton orders a cruise missile attack on the Iraqi intelligence headquarters in Baghdad, responding to the attempted assassination attempt cultivated by the Iraq Secret Service on former U.S. President George H.W. Bush during his visit to Kuwait two months before.

November 20, 1993 - The Senate Ethics Committee censures California Senator Alan Cranston for his participation with Charles Keating in the Savings and Loan scandal. The scandal had begun in the 1980s due to a wave of mismanagement, failed speculation, and fraud within the industry.

November 30, 1993 - The Brady Handgun Violence Prevention Act is signed into law by President Bill Clinton.

1994
January 1, 1994 - The North American Free Trade Agreement (NAFTA) goes into effect, creating a free trade zone between Canada, the United States, and Mexico.

June 12, 1994 - The bodies of Nicole Brown SImpson and Ronald Goldman are found outside her home in Los Angeles, California. Five days later, her husband, former football star O.J. Simpson is arrested for the crime, but is later acquitted on October 3, 1995. The Simpson case was one of the highest profile murder cases in the nation's history.

September 13, 1994 - President Bill Clinton signs the Assault Weapons Ban, which bars the use of these weapons for ten years.

September 14, 1994 - For the first time since 1904, the World Series of Major League Baseball is cancelled, this time due to a player's strike begun in August by the Major League Baseball Players Association.

October 8, 1994 - The President of the United Nations Security Council states that Iraq must withdraw its troops from the Kuwait border and cooperate with weapons inspectors. Iraq had threatened in September to withdraw their cooperation with UNSCOM inspectors, and began a deployment of Iraqi troops near the Kuwaiti border. A United States reaction to this development during the months of September and October included the deployment of its military force to Kuwait. On

October 15, Iraq began to withdraw its troops from the Kuwait region.

November 8, 1994 - The Republican revolution concludes with the midterm elections when for the first time in forty years, the party gains control of both the Senate and the U.S. House of Representatives.

1995
January 1, 1995 - The World Trade Organization (WTO) is created, replacing the General Agreement on Tariffs and Trade (GATT) formed from a series of post-war treaties on trade. The World Trade Organization is more highly structured than the previous GATT and counted seventy-six nations among its members in 1995.

January 31, 1995 - U.S. President Bill Clinton invokes emergency powers to extend a $20 billion loan to Mexico to avert a financial disaster that had begun on December 19, 1994 during a planned exchange rate correction between the Mexican peso and American dollar.

April 19, 1995 - Anarchists Timothy McVeigh and Terry Nichols explode a bomb outside the Murrah Federal Building in Oklahoma City, killing one hundred and sixty-eight people in a domestic terrorism attack.

May 11, 1995 - One hundred and seventy nations decide to extend the Nuclear Non-proliferation Treaty indefinitely.

June 29, 1995 - For the first time, the Space Shuttle Atlantis docks with the Russian space station Mir.

July 27, 1995 - The Korean War Memorial in Washington, D.C. is dedicated in ceremonies presided by President Bill Clinton and South Korean President Kim Yong-sam.

1996
June 25, 1996 - The Khobar Towers bombing in Khobar, Saudi Arabia kills nineteen U.S. military personnel, destroying the majority of a six building apartment complex that was home to the 440th Fighter Wing. It was carried out by Islamic terrorists

seeking removal of the U.S. presence in Saudi Arabia.

July 5, 1996 - At the Roslin Institute in Scotland, Dolly, the sheep, becomes the first mammal to be cloned. This begins a rampant debate on the ethics of the procedure in animals and the viability and morality of cloning in human beings.

July 19, 1996 - The Summer Olympics Games are opened in Atlanta, Geogia by U.S. President Bill Clinton. The games are positively known for the achievements of American track and field athlete Michael Johnson, who won both the 200 and 400 meter races, setting a new World Record in the 200, and for the victory of the American women's gymnastics team. These games would be marred, however, by the Centennial Park bombing of Olympic tourists on July 27, which killed one person and injured one hundred and eleven.

November 5, 1996 - President William J. Clinton defeats Republican Presidential candidate Bob Dole, as well as the second run of businessman Ross Perot. Clinton gained 49.2% of the popular vote, and increased his total in the Electoral College to 379. Dole gained 40.7% of the popular tally and 159 in the Electoral College. Perot's influence on this race was marginal compared to 1992, receiving only 8.4% of the vote in 1996.

December 5, 1996 - A speech by the Federal Reserve Board Chairman Alan Greenspan suggests that irrational exuberance may be causing the extraordinary runup of stock prices.

1997
February 9, 1997 - The Simpsons, a ribald cartoon about a family of misfits, becomes the longest running prime-time cartoon television series in history, surpassing the Flintstones.

March 4, 1997 - Federal funding for any research into human cloning is barred by President Bill Clinton.

May 25, 1997 - Strom Thurmond becomes the longest serving member of the United States Senate at forty-one years and ten months.

July 8, 1997 - The NATO alliance expands into eastern Europe when it extends an invitation to the Czech Republic, Hungary, and Poland to join the alliance in 1999.

October 29, 1997 - Iraq states that it will begin to shoot down U-2 surveillance planes used by United Nations UNSCOM inspectors attempting to mandate Saddam Hussein meet the provisions of surrender in the 1991 Gulf War.

1998
January 26, 1998 - The Monica Lewinsky scandal begins when U.S. President Bill Clinton denies his relationship with the White House intern in a televised interview. This denial, and other denials to a grand jury investigation, would lead to the impeachment of the president.

February 23, 1998 - Osama bin Laden publishes his fatwa that announced a jihad against all Jews and Crusaders. This announcement would push forward the Islamic fundamentalist agenda toward terrorism against western interests.

May 18, 1998 - The United States Department of Justice and twenty states file the anti-trust case, U.S. versus Microsoft. On November 5, 1999, a preliminary ruling stated that Microsoft had monopoly power.

August 7, 1998 - Attacks on two United States embassies in Africa, in Dar es Salaam, Tanzania, and Nairobi, Kenya kills two hundred and twenty-four and injures four thousand five hundred. The attacks are linked to Osama Bin Laden and his Al-Qaeda organization. On August 13, the United States launches cruise missile strikes against Al-Qaeda camps in Afghanistan and a suspected chemical plant in the Sudan.

September 29, 1998 - The United States Congress passes legislation, the Iraq Liberation Act, that states the U.S. wants to remove Saddam Hussein from power and replace it with a democracy.

October 29, 1998 - John Glenn, thirty-six years after becoming the first American astronaut to orbit the earth, becomes the oldest astronaut in space at seventy-seven years old. His role on the Space Shuttle Discovery flight tests the effect of space travel on aging.

1999
January 1, 1999 - The Euro currency is introduced as a competitive tool to stem the power of the dollar and maximize the economic power of the European Union nations.

February 12, 1999 - President Bill Clinton is acquitted by the U.S. Senate in the Monica Lewinsky scandal. The Senate trial, which began January 7 and needed a 2/3 majority to convict, ended with a 55-45 not guilty vote on the charge of perjury and 50-50 vote on the charge of obstruction of justice.

March 29, 1999 - The Dow Jones Industrial Average closes above 10,000 for the first time.

May 3, 1999 - A series of tornadoes strikes Oklahoma, including an F5 category storm that slams Oklahoma City, killing thirty-eight. The fastest wind speed ever recorded on earth is measured by scientists at 509 km (318 mph) during this tornado.

November 30, 1999 - The first major mobilization of the anti-globalization movement occurs in Seattle, Washington, during the days before the 1999 World Trade Organization meetings. The protests and rioting caused the cancellation of the WTO opening ceremonies.

2000

April 1, 2000 - The 2000 census enumerates a population of 281,421,906, increasing 13.2% since 1990. As regions, the South and West continued to pick up the majority of the increase in population, moving the geographic center of U.S. population to Phelps County, Missouri.

April 3, 2000 - The ruling in the case of the United States versus Microsoft states that the company did violate anti-trust laws by diminishing the capability of its rivals to compete.

June 1, 2000 - For the first time since 1851, the United States of America does not participate in a major World's Fair, the Hannover 2000 World Expo, despite a record number, 187, of international participants. President Bill Clinton had withdrawn U.S. participation late in 1999 after agreement to participate in 1997. Congressional apathy toward participation in world events continues a decline in U.S. involvement after the fall of the Soviet Union and victory in the Cold War. A consequence of this policy has led to a rise, among some experts, of anti-American sentiment and a decline of U.S. influence in diplomatic affairs. Less than half, 18.1 million, of the original attendance estimate, 40 million, visit Hannover's event.

November 7, 2000 - George W. Bush, son of the former President, and Vice President Al Gore hold a virtual dead-heat for the presidency, with a disputed vote in Florida holding off the naming of the winner of the Presidential Election until the Supreme Court of the United States voted in favor of Bush on December 12. This ruling gave Florida to the Bush camp by a 527 vote majority and a victory in the Electoral College, 271-266, despite gaining less popular votes than Gore.

November 7, 2000 - Hillary Rodham Clinton wins a seat for the United States Senate from New York. It is the first time a former First Lady wins public office.

December 28, 2000 - Montgomery Ward, the retail giant since its founding one hundred and twenty-eight years before, announces its intention to cease business. Competition from newer, low-cost retail behemoths such as Wal-Mart lead to its demise.

2001
January 6, 2001 - Certification of the Electoral College victory of the 2000 United States Presidential election in the U.S. Senate confirms George W. Bush as the victor, with Dick Cheney as his Vice-President.

April 1, 2001 - China-U.S. incident. An American spy plane collides with a fighter plane of China and makes an emergency landing in Hainan, China. The U.S. crew is detained for ten days.

April 8, 2001 - Tiger Woods becomes the first golfer to hold all four major golf titles simultaneously by winning the Master's tournament in Augusta, Georgia. This followed a remarkable run in 2000 when Woods claimed victory at the final three majors of that season; the U.S. Open, the British Open, and the PGA Championship.

September 11, 2001 - Islamic fundamentalist terrorists hijack four U.S. airliners and crash them into the Pentagon and the World Trade Center in New York City. The attack of two planes levels the World Trade Center and the crash of one plane inflicts serious damage to the Pentagon in Arlington, Virginia, causing nearly 3,000 deaths. The fourth plane is heroically crashed by passengers into a Shanksville, Pennsylvania cornfield when they learn of the plot, preventing destruction of another structure in Washington, D.C., supposed to be the White House or the Capitol building. The plot is attributed to the Al-Qaeda organization led by Osama Bin Laden.

September 18, 2001 - Anthrax attacks by mail from Princeton, New Jersey against news and government targets begin. Federal officials announce the first case on October 4.

October 7, 2001 - In response to the tragedy of September 11, the United States military, with participation from its ally the United Kingdom, commence the first attack in the War on Terrorism on the Taliban and Al-Qaeda in Afghanistan. By November 12, the Taliban government leaves the capital, Kabul.

2002

February 8, 2002 - Amid tight security due to terrorism concerns, the Winter Olympic Games are opened by President George W. Bush in Salt Lake City, Utah. They would continue without major incident until the closing ceremony on February 24.

May 21, 2002 - The United States State Department issues its report in the War on Terror. It states that there are seven nations that a State-Sponsors: Iran, Iraq, Cuba, Libya, North Korea, Sudan, and Syria.

July 5, 2002 - Continuing its pattern of the past several years, Iraq refuses new proposals from the United Nations concerning weapons inspections. The inspections were part of the cease-fire agreement and terms of surrender in the 1991 Gulf War. On September 12, U.S. President George Bush addresses the United Nations and warns the members that Iraq presents a grave danger to the world that they must confront, or that the United States and others will act unitarily. On October 2, 2002, the United States Congress passes a resolution giving the President of the U.S. the authority to use the military forces of the country as he thinks necessary.

November 8, 2002 - The United Nations passes Resolution 1441 in a unanimous Security Council vote. It forces Saddam Hussein and Iraq to disarm or face serious consequences.

November 21, 2002 - NATO invites additional members of the former Soviet bloc to join its membership. Seven nations are included in the invitation; Bulgaria, Estonia, Latvia, Lithuania, Romania, Slovakia, and Slovenia.

2003

February 1, 2003 - A tragedy at NASA occurs when the Space Shuttle Columbia explodes upon reentry over Texas. All seven astronauts inside are killed.

March 19, 2003 - The War in Iraq begins with the bombing of Baghdad after additional measures and mandates from the United Nations and the United States coalition fail to gain concessions or the removal of Saddam Hussein from power. The U.S. coalition, upon failure to extract authority from the U.N. for action due to the veto power of France, begin land operations one day later with participation from U.S., British, Australian, and Polish troops.

April 9, 2003 - The U.S. coalition seizes control of Baghdad in the Iraq conflict.

July 2, 2003 - The International Olympic Committee votes in Prague that the Winter Olympic Games are coming back to North America, selecting Vancouver, Canada as host of the XXI Olympic Games in 2010.

December 13, 2003 - Saddam Hussein, former leader of Iraq, is captured in a small bunker in Tikrit by the U.S. 4th Infantry Division.

2004
February 3, 2004 - The Central Intelligence Agency admits that the imminent threat from weapons of mass destruction was not present before the 2003 Iraq war began.

March 2, 2004 - Mars rover MER-B (Opportunity) confirms to NASA that the area of their landing was once covered in water.

July 4, 2004 - The groundbreaking ceremony for the Freedom Tower at Ground Zero, the former site of the World Trade Center complex destroyed during the September 11, 2001 attacks, occurs in New York City.

November 2, 2004 - President George W. Bush wins reelection over Democratic Senator John Kerry from Massachusetts. He wins 50.7% of the popular vote and 286 votes in the Electoral College.

December 26, 2004 - The southeast Asian tsunami occurs following a 9.3 Richter scale earthquake in the Indian Ocean. Two hundred and ninety thousand people die from Sri Lanka to Indonesia, creating one of the greatest humanitarian tragedies in history. A worldwide relief effort, led by the United States and many other nations, is mobilized to assist.

2005

May 31, 2005 - After more than thirty years in suspense, the identity of Deep Throat, the contact for reporters Woodward and Bernstein in the uncovering of the Watergate scandal, is revealed when W. Mark Felt, the second in command at the CIA at the time, confirms that he was their contact.

July 26, 2005 - In the first Space Shuttle flight since the tragedy of 2003, Discovery goes into orbit on a mission that returns to earth safely on August 9.

August 29, 2005 - Hurricane Katrina strikes the Gulf Coast, inundating the city of New Orleans with water from Lake Pontchartrain when the levees that maintain the below sea level city break. Over one thousand three hundred people perish from Alabama to Louisiana in one of the worst natural disasters to strike the United States.

October 24, 2005 - Civil Rights activist, Rosa Parks, dies.

October 26, 2005 - The War of Terror continues. With elections in Iraq to confirm a new constitution vying with internal terrorism amid the U.S. military presence on October 15, eleven days later a statement from the Iranian President, Mahmoud Ahmadinejad, calls for the destruction of Israel and condemns the peace process.

2006

February 22, 2006 - In a continuing shift of the retail industry to new platforms, it is announced that the one billionth song is downloaded from the internet music store, Apple iTunes. This shift comes at the expense of many brick and mortar chains, including Tower Records.

September 25, 2006 - In New Orleans, the Louisiana Superdome reopens after repairs caused by Hurricane Katrina damage. The repairs included the largest re-roofing project in U.S. history and took thirteen months following the destruction to the Gulf Coast region.

October 17, 2006 - The population of the United States reaches the milestone of three hundred million, taking only forty-two years to gain one hundred million people since the two hundredth million person was added in 1964. At the same time, a vibrant debate on immigration policy, particularly illegal immigration, ensues across the nation.

November 7, 2006 - In the mid-term elections, both houses of Congress change back to Democratic hands for the first time since 1994. This is seen as a referendum by many on the Iraq policy of the Bush administration as well as personal Republican scandals among some House and Senate members.

December 1, 2006 - United States manufacturing capacity and esteem wanes, signaled by the sale of the last shares of his General Motors stock by U.S. billionaire Kirk Kerkorian.

2007
January 4, 2007 - The first female speaker of the U.S. House of Representatives, Representative Nancy Pelosi of San Francisco, California, is sworn into office.

January 10, 2007 - President George W. Bush announces a troop surge of 21,500 for the war in Iraq to stem the violence at the request of new commander General Petraeus. This controversial policy begins to show positive signs once fully implemented during the summer months, with a reduction in violent attacks against coalition forces and Iraqi civilians. Progress on the political front within the Iraqi national government, however, does not keep pace with positive developments on the military front.

June 2, 2007 - A terror plot to blow up JFK International Airport in New York City is thwarted when four terrorists are arrested and charged with its plan.

July 4, 2007 - The fifty star flag of the United States of America becomes the longest flying flag in American history after flying over forty-seven years.

December 13, 2007 - The Mitchell Report on the Steroids Scandal in baseball is published. It recounted a year long investigation into the use and abuse of performance enhancing drugs over a two decade period, including steroids and human growth hormone. Nearly ninety players were named, and blame for the scandal was spread among players, the union, and the commissioner's office. Headed by former Senator George Mitchell, the report urged enhanced testing to stem the problem and a look forward attitude to restore the integrity of the game and its statistics. The report comes after a season when Barry Bonds broke the home run record of Hank Aaron amid suspicion of steroid use.

2008
July 1, 2008 - A report by the U.S. embassy in Iraq states that 15 of the 18 goals set for the Iraqi government have been met, largely due to the surge implemented over the last year. The increase of 21,500 United States troops, commonly known as the surge, reduced violence and restored order to the nation, allowing the government of Iraq to focus more on solving other problems needed to establish a stable nation.

August 17, 2008 - Michael Phelps, the United States swimmer from Baltimore, wins his 8th Gold Medal of the Beijing Summer Olympic Games, surpassing the record of seven won by Mark Spitz.

August 29, 2008 - John McCain chooses Sarah Palin, 1st term Governor of Alaska, as his running mate, making the contest between Barack Obama and himself, the first time a presidential election included both an African-American candidate and a woman amongst the Presidential and Vice Presidential nominees for president among the Democratic and Republican tickets.

October 3, 2008 - The United States Congress passes legislation, signed by President Bush, for a $700 billion bailout, the Emergency Economic Stabilization Act, giving the Treasury Department authority to assist distressed Wall Street and banking businesses of the United States due to the housing, banking, and subprime mortgage crises caused by excessive greed and speculation among Wall Street firms. This economic distress, coupled with oil prices above $140 per barrel during the summer, deepened the world economic crises that had been brewing all year. The bailout was supported by current President George W. Bush and both presidential candidates, Barack Obama and John McCain.

November 4, 2008 - Barack Obama, Democratic Senator from Illinois, the land of Abraham Lincoln, wins a landslide margin in the Electoral College, 365 to 173 in the election for the 44th President of the USA over John McCain, making him the first African-American president in the history of the United States of America.

2009
January 20, 2009 - Barack Obama takes the oath of office for President of the United States, becoming the first African-American president in the history of the nation. The Democratic Senator from Illinois comes into the office on a message of Change. The city of Washington, D.C. hosts more than one million visitors to the inauguration, covering the National Mall in a way reminiscent of the Civil Rights March of Martin Luther King forty-six years earlier.

April 15, 2009 - After a succession of big government spending projects beginning in the Bush administration and expanded under President Obama, 750 grass roots Tea Party protests spring up across the nation. More than one half million citizens concerned with increased deficits due to actions such as the bailout of the banking industry, car industry, potential cap and trade legislation, and other administration projects that project a ten trillion dollar deficit over the next decade take part.

June 11, 2009 - The H1N1 virus, named the Swine Flu, is deemed a global pandemic by the World Health Organization. This is the first such designation since the Hong Kong flu in 1967-1968.

October 31, 2009 - The economic recession continues to deepen as jobless claims climb above 10.0%, reaching 10.2% with October's monthly figures. This occurs despite efforts by the Obama administration to ramp up massive government spending pushed by the $780 billion economic stimulus package passed earlier in the year.

December 1, 2009 - President Obama announces a surge of 30,000 additional troops to Afghanistan to stem increased efforts by the Taliban in the country. The surge, which was suggested by military officers, was not popular with the liberal base of the Democratic party which had put the President in power on a pledge to end both Middle Eastern wars. The war in Afghanistan, which started as a response to the terror attacks on 9/11/2001, and the war on terror in general, comes into focus again on December 25 when an airliner headed for Detroit is attacked by a Muslim extremist, 23-year-old Umar Farouk Abdulmutallab, who attempts to detonate a bomb, but fails.

2010
January 19, 2010 - Scott Brown, a Republican reformer from Massachusetts, stuns the nation with an upset win for the special election Senate seat. He is the first Republican elected to the Senate from the state since 1972 and only Republican member of the Massachusetts Democratic congressional delegation. His election puts a halt to the 60 seat Democratic super majority in the Senate and will prevent President Obama and the Democratic leadership from pushing legislation in future votes past a Republican filibuster.

March 25, 2010 - The U.S. House of Representatives finalizes the Health Care legislation approved by the Senate, extending health benefits and insurance to most Americans. The legislation, the Affordable Care Act, passed on a partisan basis by the Democratic Majority, has caused a significant rift within the public, who disapproved of the bill, and is expected to test the Democratic Party's hold on both houses of Congress during the mid-term elections in November.

April 1, 2010 - The U.S. Census of 2010 is conducted, showing a 9.7% increase from the 2000 census for a total of 308,745,538 people. The geographic center of the population is now 2.7 miles northeast of Plato, Missouri.

April 20, 2010 - A British Petroleum deep water oil rig explodes in the Gulf of Mexico, causing the largest oil spill in the history of the United States, killing eleven workers, and devastating the environment. It also severely damaged the fishing and tourism industries of gulf states.

November 2, 2010 - With an impetus from the Tea Party movement to restore fiscal sanity to Congress and various state houses, Republican candidates win the majority of elections, taking control of the U.S. House of Representatives with a net gain of 63 seats, reducing the majority of Democrats in the Senate, and taking over many governorships and other legislative bodies. This tide was the biggest turnaround in Congressional seats since 1948, and many attribute the election to disfavor of Obama administration spending practices, including the Health Care legislation passed in March.

2011
April 14, 2011 - Congress votes to pass the 2010-2011 budget after six months of negotiations, including $38 billion in fiscal year cuts. This vote was one of the first measures that showed the new dynamic of a U.S. House of Representatives in Republican hands that was focused, due to Tea Party member goals, to get the burgeoning federal deficit under control.

May 2, 2011 - Osama Bin Laden, mastermind of the 9/11, 2001 attacks on the World Trade Center, the Pentagon, and other locations and leader of the terrorist group, Al-Queda, is killed after ten years of pursuit by United States and coalition forces during a raid by U.S. Navy Seals on his hideout location in Pakistan.

July 21, 2011 - The final shuttle flight lands at the Kennedy Space Center, signifying the end of the NASA shuttle space program. The program, which began in 1981 and included 135 missions, was completed when the Shuttle Atlantis flew its final mission to the International Space Station.

September 17, 2011 - The first of many Occupy Wall Street protests begin in New York City, protesting the big money interests on Wall Street and their relationship to the recession and world economy.

December 15, 2011 - The war in Iraq is declared over when President Obama orders the last combat troops to leave the country.

2012
May 2, 2012 - At a New York auction house, the highest payment for a work of art, the Scream by Edwin March, is paid, costing $120 million dollars.

May 7, 2012 - The first licenses for cars without drivers is granted in the state of Nevada to Google. Autonomous cars were first introduced in concept during the 1939 World's Fair in New York City in the General Motors exhibit Futurama by Norman Bel Geddes. By September of 2012, three states had passed laws allowing such vehicles; Nevada, California, and Florida.

September 11, 2012 - Terrorist attack on a consulate in the Libyan city of Benghazi kills four Americans, including Ambassador John C. Stevens, showing the continued fight against Islamic extremism had not abated after the Arab Spring uprisings in the Middle East and deposing of dictators such as Muammar Gaddafi.

October 29, 2012 - Hurricane Sandy, taking an unusual track up the East Coast and coming to landfall on the New Jersey coast near Atlantic City and Long Island coasts of New York creates significant damage to coastal towns as well as the boroughs of Manhattan and Staten Island, to the estimated cost of $65.6 billion. The hurricane, at its peak a Category 2 storm, was the largest storm in recorded history by diameter at 1,100 miles.

November 6, 2012 - President Barack Obama wins a significant victory, 332 electoral votes to 206, for his second term in office against Republican challenger and businessman Mitt Romney. Congress remained status quo with divided government as the House of Representatives remained in Republican hands and the Senate in Democratic hands.

2013
February 12, 2013 - Using a 3-D printer and cell cultures, American scientists at Cornell University grow a living ear.

April 15, 2013 - Two bombs explode near the finish line of the Boston Marathon, killing three and injuring hundreds in a terrorism attack coordinated by two brothers associated with radical Islam. The attack caused the shutdown of the city as police and federal officials searched and apprehended the suspects within four days of the attack.

May 17, 2013 - Congressional hearings begin on the IRS scandal of group targeting that began two years prior. The Internal Revenue Service is accused of targeting conservative groups for additional scrutiny in tax status matters, including groups like the Tea Party, whose stances include lower taxes and smaller government, plus other patriotic and religious organizations. This breach of protocol from a government agency where all U.S.

citizens file taxes has caused concern from both Republican, Democrat, and independent political groups.

August 28, 2013 - One hundred thousand visitors throng to the Lincoln Memorial and the National Mall in Washington, D.C. for the 50th anniversary commemoration ceremony of Martin Luther King's "I Have a Dream" speech. Speakers at the anniversary include two former presidents; Jimmy Carter, Bill Clinton, and current President Barack Obama, the first African American to hold the office. Nearly 250,000 people came to the original speech in 1963.

October 1, 2013 - The Affordable Care Act, Obamacare, begins registering people for the expanded federal government health insurance program despite a variety of waivers and problems in implementing the cumbersome rules and regulations of the program. Various states have decided to allow the federal government to run the exchanges for them, while some states and the District of Columbia set up their own exchanges to sell the policies.

Source Notes:

The information provided within this timeline was gleaned from various sources, as well as the knowledge and experience of the America's Best History staff, and should not be considered a scholarly work per se, but as a jumping off point for the reader to go into more detail about a particular topic of their interest. We would also urge you to visit the historic sites of the USA, as they will provide you with invaluable knowledge and experience into our history, no matter which subject or site you prefer. It is often the best way to add to your historic wealth of knowledge, and a whole lot more fun than you might anticipate.

Support Our Partners:

Baseballevaluation.com
Home to Stat Geek Baseball, all-time historic player ratings, and best ever lists, it provides a historic viewpoint on the numbers and past of America's pastime, from 1871 to the present day.

Teepossible.com
Official t-shirts and gifts from americasbesthistory.com and the best historic sites and national parks in the USA. Also home to Catch Phrase Mania and Top Prospect Sports. T-shirts, iPAD cases, mugs, and other gifts for fun, history, and sports.

CPSIA information can be obtained at www.ICGtesting.com
Printed in the USA
BVOW03s1044121213

338944BV00005B/12/P